Spiritual Intelligence

Human Consciousness Realized

Dianne Irene

ISBN: 1507504039
ISBN-13: 978-1507504031

DEDICATION

This is publically dedicated to the human race. We are a human race that are all part of creation. We must soon learn to live peacefully together or face extinction on many fronts. This peace must also transcend into how we treat our entire ecosystem. The balance of spirit rests in how we execute our lives now and in the future. Our choice in how we see the world will be our future.

This is personally dedicated to my husband Michael, Family including my parents Cliff and Csilla, extended family and those family members who have moved on including: my Grandmother Irene de Molnar Kalman, Grandfather Major Paul Kalman, Great Grandparents Karoly Molnar and Barbara de Molnar Weigand, Great-Great Grandparents Henrik Weigand and Magdolna Kecskes, Great-Great Grandparents Bela Kalman and Marild Lovassy. Also to my aunt Linda and uncle George Wagner, my uncle Joe Bentley Jr., my great grandmother Olive Mae, and those that I have loved both still in this timeline and those who are not. You know who you are and that love is eternal……

CONTENTS

ACKNOWLEDGMENTS

Those who have come to this conscious awareness and stood to ensure they empower humanity with their message deserve to be acknowledged. The Kubler-Ross Foundation is an excellent resource for understanding death and how it is part of life. Kubler-Ross's book, *On Death and Dying* is a great tool to share with others. *Nothing Better than Death* by Kevin Williams is a great asset to humanity. It demonstrates that there is a connection between all of us regardless of your personal beliefs. Dr. David Dosa's book *Making Rounds with Oscar* is an important glimpse into the blessing that animals are in this reality. It is a reminder that they are sentient beings.

Those that I have known personally that inspired humanity with their efforts also deserve that acknowledgement. My grandfather and grandmother believed the more you are blessed with in life then the more responsibility you have to humanity. This concept has been one of my mantras in life. They opposed Hitler and this took true courage. I am forever thankful that they did. The burden of being caught in the middle of such dark circumstances weighed heavily on their spirit. I know they wish they could have done more. My mother has been a source of unconditional love that has been a joy to my life. Before my many years of college and university education, my father encouraged my habit of research by handing me a pile of books to read when I had questions and it served as the best education. It empowered me to employ critical thinking in everything. Also, those that I have met along the way both those I can mention and those that I cannot. The intriguing government analyst, the military and government individuals that shared their hearts and lessons learned, Dr. Brian and Mer for their efforts to show and see the beauty in life, the silver moon gazer, and even those who have disagreed with me. Thank you for encouraging me, challenging me, and inspiring me. Dr. Brian O'Leary once said to me, "I want to get it right... I want to serve humanity and I won't sell out". Integrity meant a great deal to him. I am thankful for this reminder. His book *The Energy Solution Revolution* is an important reminder that we must take responsibility on this planet. Many students that I have had have also challenged me to know more and be more by their questions and curiosity. No boxes are needed and transparency is always welcome. Thank you for sharing your stories and your experiences.

OPEN TO THE JOURNEY

There is a very dire need for the human race to progress in our thoughts, beliefs, and behaviors. Our planet is one of the most beautiful planets with all the riches needed for us to co-exist in peace without greed and hate. We only need to realize that we are all on the same team and that our destructive behaviors must come to a stop if we are to see generations in the future of this planet thriving. We cannot have practices that are destructive to some and think that it will not eventually affect all of us as we are all connected.

Spiritual Intelligence is a reflection of what humanity is and what we can strive to be. Join this journey of hope and realization about the human spirit and understand what part the physical world plays in our journey to love, grow and learn. Death is not the end and our life has purpose beyond our everyday experiences.

What is consciousness? It is an awareness of life, thoughts, sense of self, and the elements of life. It is an awareness of others. It is an awareness of the sacredness of life. It is acknowledging life through thoughts, feelings, emotions, actions and reactions. Living in a state of consciousness means that there is a balance or symbiosis to how one fits into existence within the environment. It is necessary to understand how we exist in the physical world as an expression of a much bigger existence. Our physical expression of ourselves is only part of who we are.

Spirit is not meant as a religious term. The spirit is the part that makes us animated. It is the immortal part of us. Even if we are removed or disconnected from our current bodies we would then experience reality without them. The point here is that we are not our bodies and they are not the truest part of us. We are much more in the sense of creation. We are immortal spirits living in a flesh reality until we wear out or are separated from that body.

Some people have realized this truth after a near death experience (NDE) where they were able to bring back memories of a glimpse of what is beyond the veil of the physical realm. Some of us are sensed to be old souls and young souls and this is not that far from the truth. As immortal beings, we will not be destroyed and will live on from the time we are created.

Chapter 1
PHILOSOPHY AND PSYCHOLOGY

In many cultures today, we have focused on intellectual intelligence. We have transformed our education systems to measure whether our children know certain facts in history, logic, and communications. We no longer focus on the higher intelligence that Aristotle, Di Vinci, Tesla, and even Einstein later in his life realized was the highest form of intelligence. This is spiritual intelligence. Some attempt to describe part of this with what is called emotional intelligence, but this is only a part of the picture. We need to go deeper to the human spirit to understand our true purpose of being.

Science, in the last century has attempted to assign all pertinent information through a process of the scientific method. If information was not able to fit this model then it was rejected as important information. However, science has since made a turn back to philosophy. Philosophy was really the first modern field of psychology and an origin of understanding the mind manifested from spirit. The development of psychology was done in an effort to make the understanding of human nature a science. However, in an attempt to modernize this field, the human spirit was neglected. Aristotle, Di Vinci, and other philosophers did not need a scientific method to explore the animated part of the human existence in the physical form. They also understood that science without the understanding of the spiritual realm was only the framework of a partially empty process. Just as the art of psychology (vs. the science of psychology) has been considered an insult to the field, spiritual intelligence has been considered a leap into a place of uncertainty and to some a pseudo-psychology (fake). `However, philosophy was the origin of psychology. The transition into psychology was made to make science the focus of the mind and its components. However, consciousness cannot be put into a mechanical scientific method and adhere to a political academic regimen.

In early psychology, there was a wavering in explaining human thought. Introspection was coined by Wilhelm Wundt and later the onset of behaviorism by John Watson became a focus. Then there was the eccentric view of Freud that has been rejected by some contemporaries. However, we have seen a transition into a more eclectic view of psychology. Just as we have experienced a downturn of many great societies who become too involved in politics and power, it has been because of the loss of concern of the human element. The human element includes the empathy and concern for humanity and how we interact with our environment. It also has origins in recognizing an animated part of each living being. This can only be completely understood by including the spirit.

Much of human behavior is a manifestation of expression in the physical form which was designed to allow us to experience life in this dimension. What philosophy understood was that the laws of dimension trumped the laws of the physical realm. This is something that science has begun to understand. Science is beginning a transformation and is becoming more philosophical. Science is also embracing the idea that the supernatural is actually natural. Quantum physics and technological advances are shedding some light on energy in more than just a mechanical way. Humanity is now more closely focusing on a balance of physical reality and spiritual presence.

Humanity has made its way through the days of many gods, the dark ages, Victorian times, and through witch's trials, wars, and holocausts. Superstitions created a framework that humans chose to live by and then man pondered philosophy through those who understood the need for some logic in a creative mind and explored religions. Then man gravitated towards using a science to explain life and understand purpose. Humanity also stormed the earth with a predatory nature and put aside a balanced way of living with nature for what can be considered low developmental energies. These energies are seeded in fear, greed, selfishness, misuse of power and hate. Now, we have come to a place as a human race where it is time for us to see that a balance is necessary between understanding the physical realm and the spiritual realm. The animated part of us has the capacity to love, create, express joy, and inspire others. This part of us cannot be subject to the scientific method, but lends itself to a higher place in consciousness where we understand that our spiritual evolution requires embracing who we are in this reality. This also sheds a light on the realization that beyond this reality there are other factors to consider.

Human History *Overview*

Here is a brief overview of human history. While not every event can be covered, this gives a view of human progression for the purpose of seeing a bigger picture.

Prehistoric and Ancient Times

Human Progression (Spiritual, Cultural and Social)

Neanderthals rise and disappear, Homo sapiens are found. High separation of power and the masses ensures control. About 3000 BC Sumerian Cuneiform begins human recorded history and later Stonehenge is built. They contain creation stories, the stories of Adamu and Ti-amat. The stories of ancient male and female god rulers are prevalent. Multiple gods, ancient religions, superstitions manifest in pleasing the gods. A sacrifice of human and animal life to appease the gods is common. "Gods" first in Sumer and later found in the establishment of Egypt, Greece, Africa and the Middle East, South America, India and China, and Rome. Sumerian war of the gods is discussed in Sumerian history. Skeletons that were found were unique and some were giants.

Environment and Health

Alchemy and herbs are used. Population spreads throughout the world. The planet is pristine. During war of the gods a great poison cloud spreads over parts of the earth. Mining operations took place. Humans wish for immortality of the gods.

Innovation and Education

Ancient Technology of the "gods" is found in ancient writings, architecture, and artifacts. Pyramids and ancient structures start to appear all over the planet. Ancient drawings and figurines of flying machines and other technology were part of the culture, but were only used by the "gods". The "gods" educate a select few and they become priests or royal. Some offspring were relished between the "gods" and common man.

Dark Ages

Spiritual and Social Factors

Superstitions manifest in good and bad. The idea of "gods" goes to the background and religions are the direct line to God and the only safety away from evil. "Gods" handed off power to priests and rulers. The idea of the trinity begins. There was a great war of religions between the Catholic and Protestant philosophy. There was a constant struggle for power between royals and religious leaders in Europe. The royals married within the family to preserve their bloodline. This led to some recessive consequences. The fall of Rome takes place. Women become subordinates. Individuals are beheaded or mutilated because of the breaking of rules.

Witches are burned. Christianity began in the 1st century. A great power struggle occurs. Hinduism was established in India and then the Buddhist religion is established at the end of about 5th century. The establishment of Islam occurred in the 7th century and later Judaism.

Environment and Health
Plagues are an issue. Disease can be seen as a punishment from God. Alchemy and herbs are used. Life span is short for most. A great gap exists in the wealthy and poor.

Innovation and Education
Most of education was for men and those of certain class structures. Most could not read or write. This made it difficult for people to educate themselves. Poets and artists are relished.

Age of Philosophy

Spiritual and Social Factors
The idea of one God becomes prevalent. There is a move away from superstition. Reason becomes a focus rather than rules. Some saw this as enlightenment. Royals still reigned openly. The arts were a strong form of entertainment.

Environment and Health
Alchemy and herbs are used with the beginning of technology of the common people expanding. The scientific method is embraced. Farmers, blacksmiths, and skilled trades are common.

Innovation and Education
Education becomes a focus. Philosophy, art, and emerging technology are put to exploration. Slavery in Africa and United States is pervasive.

Science/Technology Age

Spiritual and Social Factors
The spiritual development is stifled. Greed becomes the addiction that pervades humankind. Religions are used for agendas of modern desire. Priests and preachers are seen with flaws. The beginning of breaking away from religion and exploration into the spiritual begins to spread. Power is oppressive and predatory. Women gain some ground and slavery and social inequality "ends" for some, but begins for others. Population explodes, but many are killed in wars. WWI and WWII bring discrimination and genocides. Hitler, himself a Jew, kills millions of Jews and many others. Hitler strips many of royal titles. Hitler strives to breed a superior race. Many royals become commoners, but still are in influential positions today.

The Chinese holocaust or Nanjing Massacre occurs between Japan and China. Communist holocaust, Stalin's cannibals, famine, and takeovers kill millions. African slaves are freed in the United States, while many other slaves still in Africa and other parts of the world are enslaved. Entertainment becomes commercial. The new "religion" is politics and people are divided into parties. This serves as another form of separation.

Environment and Health

Industrialization causes the planet great harm. Nuclear experiments on the ground and in the upper atmosphere take place. Mining is done with chemicals and industrial development causes pollution. Environmental disasters such as Chernobyl, Three Mile Island, the Great Garbage Patch, and oil spills endanger life. Mass agricultural production increases pests and the need for pesticides. Animals become a mass production product to be used for food. Introduction of GMO (strands of viruses and other materials inserted into plant DNA) foods by a chemical company. Chemical production booms. A strong move away from the natural occurs and a move towards synthetic chemicals. There is also a growing push for natural medicines and health freedom. Technology aids health, but now there are more toxins and poisons in the environment and modern medicines. Life span is longer for some.

Innovation and Education

Technology and Science advance. Development is rapid, but it does not balance with ethical considerations. The conveniences make life easier. Choices in energy and goods are not ultimately based on sustainability, but profit. Consumerism explodes. Technology aids war and innovation. Instead of altruistic development, most technology is developed for military applications before it reaches the general population. Governments become concerned about their own people and wish to see what is hidden and surveillance of citizens becomes common.

Present

Spiritual and Social Factors

Consumerism is a way of life for some. Human trafficking is a multi-billion dollar industry and still enslaves millions. To some religion is sovereign over human life and they engage in hate. Some cultures still suppress women. Fear and greed are still the dominate factors keeping humans separated. Wars are still predatory and not just for defense and have political influences. Discrimination still exists between schools of thought on religion, health care, and politics. Humans are starting to see beyond political parties and see the issues as a bigger factor over the culture of parties. Massive debt ensues. There is much debate over population control.

Environment and Health
There is a split in schools of thought in how we live in harmony with each other and the planet. Herbal medicine is outlawed in some areas and embraced in others. There is a shift to become sustainable by some while others consume more or create more consumerism. Humans consume mass amounts of animal flesh in unsustainable ways. Hunger, poverty, water, and disease are major factors. Natural resources are becoming privately owned instead of belonging to all people.

Innovation and Education
Science is becoming open to realms outside of traditional understanding. Humans realize that the scientific method cannot be applied to the human spirit. Students have free education in some countries and in others pay large amounts for education and accumulate great debt. Science is on the cusp of "immortality". Sports players are paid millions while teachers don't make enough to pay their school loans.

Possible Ideal Future
Spiritual and Social Factors
We are co-creators of the Creator. The Creator is not separated from humans by human religion. All life is seen as sacred. Love and growth is our ultimate goal. Men and women's complementary powers ensure peace and balance on earth. Nazism like behaviors cannot be repeated because a true checks and balances that exists and humans are consciously involved in governing themselves. War is only true self defense and all other matters are dealt with diplomatically. We shift from money to resources where water, land, and food are sacred rights of all people and animals. Independent farming and communities are encouraged. Humans are not part of a debt process.

Environment and Health
Humans have achieved balance in energy, power, culture, and sustainable living takes precedence over greed and power. Responsible procreation is part of the culture. Health care is personally determined and health is not based on profit. Both holistic medicine and allopathic medicine work hand in hand without regard of profit and power to ensure health over profits. Humans achieve complete health. The environment plays into development.

Innovation and Education
Science is balanced with the philosophical; the supernatural is natural, spiritual advancement through personal responsibility, understanding that

the hierarchy of dimensional reality is vast and infiltrates the understanding of the physical realm and the spiritual realm. Education is free and open. We have abandoned nuclear proliferation and non renewable resources. Energy independence is realized. We have learned to traverse the distance of space.

These cultures and societies were created by leaders. The framework for these societies were laid by "gods", religious leaders, politicians, rulers, and the wealthy. Now, it is time for all of humanity to be actively participating in how the human culture evolves. We must do this by leading ourselves and understanding the implications of how power is used.

Types of Intelligence

We begin our journey by assessing types of intelligence. Intelligence has been confined to a very narrow view in modern society. Intelligence that generates money, power, and fame has been prized as a sign of true success. This has been accepted as a means to propagate our society. However, this narrow understanding has led to a confining of the human spirit and an obstacle to spiritual maturity for the human community.

Howard Gardner (1983) proposed a list of nine types of intelligence. Gardner's ability to recognize the various aspects of intelligence was an essential part of realizing the lack of educational appropriateness in our education framework. Humans are more than just a mechanical brain able to remember, process, and apply information. Gardner's recognition of the types of intelligence opened the gateway to explore further. They are Linguistic, Logical or Mathematical, Musical, Bodily/Kinesthetic, Spatial, Naturalist (discernment of living things and nature), Intrapersonal (understanding yourself), Interpersonal (understanding others), and Existential (philosophical) intelligence (Garnder, 2003).

While some types of intelligence holds equal value to individuals, there is a hierarchy to intelligence. The IQ is measured by standard methods of education. However, this is a small part of human intelligence. Let us take a look at the traditional theories of power and intelligence. Then we can discuss how spiritual intelligence fits into the picture. We will start with how leadership uses power and intelligence.

The Use of Power in Intelligence

The use of power in a leadership role is a multi-faceted process. Understanding the types of power available and the tactics that support them can create a more efficient leadership role. It also greatly effects how others behave. Understanding is essential to the seeing the bigger picture of how leadership trickles down and frames organizations, communities, and ultimately society. Ethical leadership can be reflected in the use of power and the motivations that are utilized by that power. Locus of control, Machiavellian Personality, and Narcissism assists in defining leadership performance. Myers-Briggs Type Leaders (MBTI) can reveal responses to leadership and predict certain outcomes and successes. The use of power, influence, and tactics are aspects of leadership that can empower workers and leaders to create an interaction that leads to resolving some common issues. Understanding these factors can create a strategy for success. Understanding where these factors can be inappropriate can also ensure that a strategy can be found to re-center the leadership perspective.

Power

Power is an essential part of leadership. The use of this power can greatly affect the outcomes of communication and processes. Tactics are used to express power and strategically influence outcomes and responses. Understanding how personality influences perspective and performance assists leaders in making decisions about people and the appropriate use of power needed to elicit results.

Types of Leaders

There have many types of leadership displayed throughout history and some have achieved great feats while others have left a legacy of treachery or harm. There are some distinct differences in these leaders that centers on their emotional and spiritual maturity, their effective communication, and the ability to empower others. Some leaders have varying motivations and perspectives. Other leaders show varying levels of personal responsibility and empathy towards others.

Locus of Control

A leader's perspective of control can affect how they approach various situations. There are two basic locus of control perspectives. Leaders that have an internal locus of control have the perspective that they have control over what happens because of their actions. These types of leaders tend to take more risks and be more proactive in their behaviors (Nahavandi, 2009, p. 130). While they tend to be less anxious they will also tend to be less conforming. Leaders that have the perspective of an external locus of control tend to see their environment as a result of an outer influence. They tend to be "more reactive" in situations, rely on the judgments of others, and can be over controlling (Nahavandi, 2009, p. 130). Those that are prone to an ILC (Internal Locus of Control) are proactive, have a more resistant reaction to stress, have stronger ethical concerns are self-confident and influential. Those with an ELC (External Locus of Control) are more reactive, seek approval from others, can over react, project their own concerns on others and be domineering.

A factor that can also affect a leader's performance can be based in their perceptive of obstacles. A positive or negative outlook can reflect in the resolution strategy of the leader. Two basic personality categories consist of a Type A or Type B. Type A individuals are concerned with time, desire control, and can be inpatient with delays. They also tend to be more competitive, set higher goals, and have high energy. Type B personalities have less of a desire for control, enjoy working in groups, and delegate better than type A's (Nahavandi, 2009, p. 133). Another consideration in leadership is the ability of the leader to monitor their behavior and correctly evaluate the reality of that behavior. A self-monitoring (SM) scale was developed by in 1974 and indicated that those who had a high SM would tend to be more consistent in their behavior and have a better ability to analyze a situation (Nahavandi, 2009, p. 134).

Myers-Briggs Type Leaders (MBTI)

The Myers-Briggs testing is based on the research of Carl Jung in the 1920's. One might wonder what motivated a man to create a strong foundation in the field of psychology that laid the framework for personality testing. Carl Jung had a NDE after a heart attack and this will be further discussed later in this book. MBTI focuses on decision making as it relates to personality dimensions. These dimensions are, "sensing/intuition and thinking/feeling" and "perception/judgment and extrovert/introvert" (Nahavandi, 2009, p. 136). A pattern has been seen in various types of individuals. Those that score consistently in certain categories tend to display similar characteristics in their use of leadership skills. According to Jung, when individuals better understand themselves, their behaviors and tendencies, then they will better understand how that impacts others. They will then better comprehend how to change their behavior so they can be more effective leaders (Wall, 2008).

Sensation Thinkers are concerned with facts, quickly reactive, they like predictability, and are generally time oriented. Intuitive Thinkers are concerned with relationships, optimistic, tend to solve problems; they may have unrealistic or high expectations, analytical and intellectual. Sensation Feelers have an organized inclination, works well within rules, and prefers systems and lives in the present. Intuitive Feelers have charisma, adjusts to change, open minded, people oriented, but can get exhausted (Nahavandi, 2006).

Machiavellian Personality & Narcissism

The Machiavellian Personality is based on the extent that a leader puts their own concerns above the concerns of others. Those who score high for this personality tend to be manipulative, lack honesty, be cynical and use personal gain above the interest of the group or company. Those who score low for this personality may tend to be naïve and more easily manipulated (Nahavandi, 2009, p. 137). It would be best for leaders to not score at the extreme of being too concerned with themselves or lacking enough concern for their contribution. Another focus of self concern is the level of narcissism. Here again, those who score high for this trait tend to be selfish and self- absorbed (Nahavandi, 2009, p. 138).

Power & Influence

There are several kinds of power that leaders use to interact with their subordinates. According to French and Raven (1968) there are five main types of power which include: legitimate, reward, coercive, expert, and referent (Nahavandi, 2009, p. 63). Legitimate power is seen when a leader is in a position and is expected to hold the power. A CEO or other leader in a company is seen to hold the power and this position will give the appearance of power. Reward power is seen by others as a chance to access rewards that are held by a person in power. Perhaps a young executive will listen closely to a more experienced leader to model their behavior and gain access to the benefits of those behaviors. Coercive power is used with a result of punishment. Sales staff that must meet a quota can see the failure to reach a goal as a lingering punishment of loss of pay or position. Expert power is seen in those who hold knowledge in an area. The resident scientist of an organization can be seen as an expert in a subject and their opinion is then likely to be taken at face value. Referent power is seen in those that others are attracted to and that have relationships with others (Nahavandi, 2009, p. 63). Charismatic leaders can utilize referent power by charming workers into accomplishing a task or goal.

Tactics

Tactics are used by leaders to influence their subordinates and obtain desired results. The British Psychological Society (2007) discovered that there is a connection between some tactics used in leadership roles. It was discovered that "upward appeals" could be seen as pressures to form an alliance with someone who held more power. This might be used well in a situation when an assistant worker has to form a relationship with a leader and needs to rely upon attention to detail.

In an exchange tactic an exchange with teams and the expectation of something in return is utilized. Perhaps a reward or bonus could be used to inspire success in a team. When workers feel that they do not receive recognition or reward then this tactic will assist in bringing the team back into a positive performance mode. It is also important then to honor those promised rewards or incentives. Not doing so can create hostility in the team and cause dissention.

When "ingratiation" is used the leader is charming the others into a positive mood and attempting to influence the perception of their performance as a leader. An Inspirational appeal is valued as a commitment to others. This could be used to inspire a team as they set out to work on a new goal or to improve a certain process. When "inspirational tactics" are used there is a personal connection and is used well in consultations (Steensma, H. 2007). This would be appropriate when a worker is in need of a review or to address a concern.

The use of "rationality" uses logical and factual information to request a task or goal completion. When people are introduced to change a lack of understanding can cause dissention. By using facts and information to back up a logical action, teams can conceptualize the importance of that change. The motivations behind tactics should be considered. Research done by Eveleth & Pillutla (2003) indicated that tactics work best when leaders are successful at convincing others that there is a problem and that a solution needs to be found. They also discovered that the best tactic is when influence works best when there is an exchange and dialogue with persuasion.

Empowering

Empowering others is an essential part of leadership. Delegating enough power to others so that they feel vested in group goals and processes will increase team success. It is appropriate to create boundaries and expectations related to the goals and not to create an emphasis on control. Leaders must be visionary and be able to see many perspectives. Empowering others means that leaders must display the same commitment that they expect from their employees. Using tactics appropriately will increase the empowerment process and ensure that teams are working towards the same goals.

While many factors contribute to understanding power and the types of leadership behaviors it is also important to remember that no single test or factor can give the clearest picture of predictable behavior. According to Bud Baker, Ph.D., one test cannot give a complete assessment of a leader. Interviews are added to balance the understanding of a leader (2008). It is important to remember that these are merely guideline predictors and not snapshots of reality. Many factors go into the use of power, tactics, and understanding how all of these elements fit together could be the strongest indicator of how someone uses power successfully.

The very basis of corruption in leadership is spear headed by the lack of emotional intelligence and spiritual maturity. In early stages of development, humans discover that certain reactions to situations can elicit certain results. In infancy, humans learn that crying can get attention or food. In adolescence humans discover that they can further use responses to elicit specific reactions with greater accuracy and a refining of what was learned becomes a process of uncertainty and deeper emotional responses. By adulthood, the cycle of behaviors and responses should be balanced and encompass a self-aware individual capable of empathy, understanding, and a sense of appropriateness.

On another level, this process can face a "disjuncted" development where a dispersement of energy goes in both a positive and negative direction. This struggle is between the use of power and empowerment. In the early development stages of discovery, power is used to communicate and express basic human emotions. As a person matures, the power can be internalized and thus become a focus of self-preservation. This focus can lead to greed, manipulation, and poor judgment. Relevance and perspective are fine tuned emotional maturity components. They become the markers for appropriateness much like a compass is for direction. Any breakdown of these development factors can lead to a person's misguided decision making.

In adulthood, the sense of personal responsibility should already have been established. Otherwise, the transition into this can be difficult and the growth beyond the victim perspective can be very challenging. Psychologists have found that those leaders who scored low on emotional intelligence displayed the poorest ability to make decisions (Tasler et al., 2009). They are the leaders who do not take responsibility for their own actions and do not have a strong understanding of their own feeling and emotions (Nahavandi, 2006).

Emotional Intelligence

In early stages of development, humans discover that certain reactions to situations can elicit certain results. In infancy, humans learn that crying can get attention or food. In adolescence humans discover that they can further use responses to elicit specific reactions with greater accuracy and a refining of what was learned becomes a process of uncertainty and deeper emotional responses. By adulthood, the cycle of behaviors and responses should be balanced and encompass a self-aware individual capable of empathy, understanding, and a sense of appropriateness. Understanding our emotions and the origin of emotions is an essential part of our spiritual maturity. Psychology has recognized emotional intelligence related to understanding emotions and expressing the correct emotions for a situation. Psychology has also recognized that a person's ability to recognize the emotions of others contributes to emotional intelligence and leads to maturity.

Understanding Power

The understanding of power as a means to get a desired response on a juvenile level leads to an internalized motivation with a lack of understanding the connection in relationships and the importance they have on the spirit. The spirit can be understood as the part that makes a person animated. Beyond the physical expression is that place where people process information and create judgments about those thoughts. These become expressions of feelings. Then, actions are expressed through emotion. Anger is a feeling, but crying or yelling could be the emotional response. Learning to express appropriate emotions are also essential to the learning process. A lack of understanding and empathy will take leaders to a place where they will not relate to others. At the core of our animation, we create thought that gives birth to feeling, emotions, and actions or reactions. The spirit is capable of connecting and creating love and it transcends the physical. This process is part of the development of spiritual intelligence. The animated part of us has the power to create from thought. It is also the place where we are conscious and it exists separate from our physical form. Beyond even emotional intelligence spiritual intelligence creates our entire outlook on life and has the power to also trump current states in lower forms of intelligence. The current worldwide financial crisis has been a strong example of this lack of empathic process of relating to others. A few became greedy internalizing their power and costing the global economy to subsequently falter.

Those individuals who have a missing component in these development factors will display disconnected decisions. They will function much like a computer that has a virus or one that is missing some scripts. The development process of the human consciousness is imperative to its performance and its proactive abilities in leading appropriateness. We can refer to those in a position of leadership for an example. Since a leader's behavior has a trickle down affect on team members and subordinates, the emotional intelligence of that leader can create an environment that then becomes a framework for everyone involved. TalentSmart psychologists found that emotional intelligence will indicate how one understands their own feelings and how they read others and react accordingly (Tasler et al., 2009).

However, even team members who are functioning at higher levels of emotional maturity can revert back to a lower level of functioning due to a hostile or inappropriate environment. Therefore it is a very important responsibility of the leader to ensure an appropriate environment and take responsibility. A group of Psychologists at TalentSmart point out that when leaders take responsibility and are able to make a difficult situation into something positive then they will be the most effective decision makers (Tasler et al, 2009). Former President Lincoln apparently took this seriously and was able to even win over those who were his rivals. An opponent of Lincoln, William Seward was appointed as secretary of state and after some time working together came to respect Lincoln as a leader (Coutu, 2009).

Competition

A sense of competition is another factor in developing emotional intelligence. Leaders of our planet must properly assess their place in the perspective of competition. In our lower stages of development, competition is for preservation and develops a place where comparison is basic. Some leaders enjoy competition. It is the motivation behind the competition that determines it appropriateness. Those leaders that see their subordinate team members as sources of competition will hinder the group development. This is a practice of using power over others rather than empowering their team to a mutual growth and benefit. Situations will arise of uncertainty and when leaders are not developed and not interested in competing with themselves for higher standards, they can revert to a lower level of thought processes. Our social condition can greatly affect these processes. This can feed dynamics where others are resistant to change and they may even act against change. Those that better understand themselves and act accordingly will create an environment where others are more likely to support each other. (Gardenswartz, L. et al. 2009).

Chapter 2

SPIRITUAL INTELLIGENCE

Manifesting	
Spiritual Intelligence	At the core of our animation, we exist in thought that gives birth to feeling, emotions, and actions or reactions. It is capable of connecting and creating love and it transcends the physical. It is the highest form of intelligence that has a trickledown effect on all areas of our physical existence and is based in consciousness. It is the higher consciousness of our animation.
Dimensional Intelligence	The understanding of the natural world in relation to the spiritual world. Being sensitive to the presence of the spiritual aspects of reality. Ex. Sensitives and intuitives.
Discerning Intelligence	The ability to understand situations and the perspectives of each factor and the appropriate place for each factor in the situation. Philosophers are strong in discernment or wisdom. The wisdom to understand what the higher principle is in situations.
Emotional Intelligence	Leaning to constrain emotional expressions to an appropriate context. Learning to read other's emotions and respond accordingly.
Creative Intelligence	Music, art, theatre, and creative expression. It is a form of creation. .
Processing/ Functional	
Strategic /Logical Intelligence	The ability to manipulate information into an active process of interaction- When this is used in a negative way we see these individuals as predator like and very manipulative. In a positive way they are those who improve systems. Problem solving, Spatial Manipulation, etc.
Physical Intelligence	The ability to control and utilize the body and the interaction of objects with the body in space.
IQ (Intellectual Intelligence)	Math computations, grammar, factual information related to history, memorization and storage of facts in the long term memory and the retrieval of such.

Intelligence Hierarchy (Irene, Dianne 2012)

Notice that modern society focuses on the IQ form of intelligence on the hierarchy scale as a basis for education. This intelligence is more of a processing function much like a computer can correctly process information. It is a functional intelligence. An individual can have great intellectual intelligence, but could be found to lack "common sense" emotional or spiritual intelligence. However, when an individual has a strong spiritual and emotional, or creative intelligence then intellectual intelligence is complementary.

An individual can have various strengths in each or most of these types of intelligence. All can be strengthened by some level of instruction; however, some natural ability of the spirit can play a role in that development. This development is reflective of the condition of our arrival into this timeline. Others can be based on what necessitates experience factors for this lifetime. For example, a child with Down's syndrome has been found to have little control of emotions, but can display a great capacity to love. This is a result of a spirit condition and not a physical one or one of emotional intelligence. These individuals are here to teach humanity how to remember some of the simple things in life, but also to see the profound capacity of love. No judgment should be made on those who appear to lacking in IQ. Instead, all people play a role for a reason.

How do we begin to develop spiritual intelligence? How do we begin to replace the dysfunctional parts of ourselves and replace them with more refined and appropriate spiritual path? One of the best places to being developing spiritual intelligence is to incorporate the universal truths into understanding. This means that certain superstitions or biases will need to fall away. Open mindedness is essential to the process.

The Power of Thought

We are not our thoughts, but they are things. This statement will be a foreign concept to some as we are often taught that our brains are like computers that process thoughts and information. The mind and the brain are separate and function to serve different purposes. The brain is the mechanical part of our physical structure and our mind is the "space" where we interact between the physical and the spiritual.

Thoughts are powerful and can create reactions in our lives, seed action, and even change a choice. However, we are not our thoughts. Thoughts can be random, analyzed, and created. Experiences come from these thoughts. As we learn and grow we can learn to channel thoughts into appropriate uses. Our spirit is superior to our thoughts. The spirit is the spark of us that exists beyond our thoughts, feelings, and beliefs. The spirit is the animated part of us that lives beyond this dimension. Everything below our spirit in this hierarchy is manifested as a physical being. This means that thoughts are manifest in this dimension and they exist separate from our spirit. Imagine your entire life that you believe the earth is flat. Because you believe this your behavior is adjusted to match your belief. When you are offered a boat ride to the end of the earth, you refuse to go. Your thoughts that have given birth to this belief would be, "The earth must be flat because the scientists say that it is and others accept that it is. I will be cautious of this so that I do not fall off'. These thoughts can be at the subconscious level and sometimes we need to dig to find what our thoughts are. Once we identify them, then we can make judgments on their accuracy. Often times, thoughts give birth to our beliefs and we become so embedded in the emotional aspects of our feelings that we will even become defensive in order to preserve them.

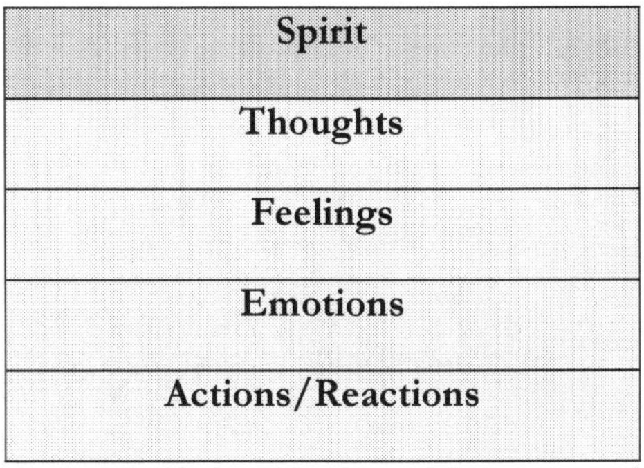

Spirit
Thoughts
Feelings
Emotions
Actions/Reactions

Physical Manifestation from Spirit (Irene, Dianne 2004)

A spirit is manifested and sent to a human form. When a spirit is born into this physical realm, it obtains many of the resources within the human expression and its environment. Many who have had a NDE (Near Death Experience) will describe how they feel stripped away of emotion, feeling, and all the manifested assets of the human form before experiencing their pure spirit form.

In some aspects, we have positive thoughts coming from our essence and thus we feel peace about them. There are times when our thoughts present themselves as dark and disjointed. It is then the responsibility of the spirit to assess those thoughts and determine what they mean. Random thoughts have become a more usual part of our spirit process. We are exposed to images, advertisements, and perspectives. We are influenced by a bombardment of negative representations of reality. This influence can cause humans to be either pushed to realization or subdued by their presence.

Emotions and Feelings

Emotions are expressions that manifest themselves into a physical reality. They can be seen as crying and physical expressions of anger like shouting or violence. They can also be seen as a sullen expression of sadness. Feelings are the states behind the emotions. A person might be crying, but feeling any of several feelings like anger or sadness. It is important to understand the difference between feeling and emotion in the hierarchy of our manifested selves.

	Feelings	Emotions
Fear	One of the most basic feelings. It should only be used in circumstance requiring life saving behavior and can trigger the flight or fight response.	Inappropriate emotional expression, withdrawal from growth, relationship, and courage. Reactionary and higher thought process can become latent.
Anger	Anger is like the daughter of fear and is often manifested as a result of pain	Anger expressed- crying, physical violence, moping
Sadness	Disappointment manifested	Crying, depression, etc.
Happiness	Embracing and elation of a desire of the physical or interaction from the outside in	Laughter, excitement, etc.
Joy	A source of elation from the inside out	Laughter, crying, etc.
Peace	Peace brings about an equilibrium between our existence of the physical and spiritual	Stable expressions in the physical

Feeling and Emotions (Irene, Dianne 2004)

Pain

There is physical pain and emotional pain. Physical pain renders our nervous system in overdrive and we seek to escape this sensation. When you touch a hot stove, you quickly move your hand away from the hot stove. This pain serves to tell us when something should be avoided. It also serves to tell us that something is wrong. If you are running and suddenly your ankle hurts, then you know that something has happened. Your ankle could be broken or some tissue could be damaged. This tells you that you must rest or you are in need of healing.

Emotional pain indicates that there is an imbalance and we should seek to rebalance. Some humans incorrectly process this and can sometimes seek out emotional pain to compensate for another emotional pain. This can contribute to an addiction. When the pain is not brought back to a homeostasis state then the person becomes unstable emotionally and growth does not take place.

Positive Growth	⟺	**Regression**
Love	Pain	Fear- can manifest in control factors
Remorse	Pain	Guilt
Peace	Pain	Chaos, war, aggression, anger
Gratitude	Pain	Selfishness, greed, gluttony
Kindness, Tolerance	Pain	Judgment
Productivity	Pain	Laziness
Empowerment	Pain	Control, Dominance
Justice	Pain	Vengeance
Goodness	Pain	Manipulation

Pain Perspective (Irene, Dianne 2007)

Feelings which express in the physical as emotions are made up of energy. Each has a unique energy. Perhaps, sometime in the distant future we will learn to read these energies the way we now read words. The positive emotions emit a higher frequency and the negative emotions emit a lower frequency. Higher frequencies lead to growth and balance. Low energy leads to a victim/predator cycle of regression.

Pain is an active force of fear. Behind the thoughts of pain, they will break down to thoughts that correlate with a fear. Think about someone who has experienced a great deal of stress and emotional pain. Some are sensitive enough to be effected by simple everyday frustrations. They become triggers for a deep reservoir of lingering pain. For example, a woman who had a very critical father will have a short tolerance for men later in her life because of left over un-healed pain. In therapy, we will find that her thoughts may be, "The criticism is an indication of rejection". Once that pain of rejection is realized in term of a fear of rejection, then healing can occur.

Secrecy Verses Transparency

Secrecy has kept humanity from progressing in several ways. While we currently live in an environment where secrecy has been heralded as a way to protect and control information, people, and cultures, it has also kept humanity from progression. This concept is in fact so progressive that some are threatened by the very concept. It means that monetary wealth, technological advancements, and trade secrets would be threatened according to current standards. Humanity must eventually realize that it is our environmental factors that are flawed and must someday change if we are ever to progress in our spiritual evolution.

Secrecy is actually a weakness when considering the other side of the coin. Imagine a race that creates advancements and then freely shares it with humanity. Where would their weakest link be? Their energy would be spent on the next advancement and not on maintaining control of a particular advancement. When we tap into truth, it does not mean that we really own it or even created it. Truth, advancement, empowerment all belong to humanity and it is really awareness that brings about the realization of these things.

Humanity has a pool of momentum that can progress or regress. Looking at physics we see that everything has an energy which creates a momentum. While one person making a ripple in this momentum can seem unnoticeable, it actually creates energy that seeks to move forward. Looking at a person who is always seeing the negative side of situations will serve as an example of this type of momentum. Then we must consider the momentum of someone who sees the opportunity in situations and how they create a momentum. Then, if we were to multiply this momentum it works much like the concept of multiplicity.

Humanity needs to ask: which momentum would we like to create? Sometimes we get so caught up in our cultures that we forget that humanity is a spiritual community. From a higher perspective humanity has unison. As an example, we can consider the human body. If your brain wishes to keep a secret from your leg, then your leg cannot function as its highest level. If your leg wishes to keep a secret from your brain then, function will be impaired. The human "body" works the same way. We can only be as great as the least of ourselves in a community. In our culture, we use the predator prey mentality to justify the current system. In reality, the secrecy and control produce low energy momentum. Instead, empowerment and transparency create a high energy momentum.

Energy Momentum	
Power/Control	Empowerment/ Transparency
lower energy momentum	higher energy momentum
Regression- Fear	Progression- Love

Energy Momentum (Irene, Dianne 2009)

Control and secrecy bring about fear factors which is also a low energy wave source. Those who live by fear cannot progress and give up their ability to think in conjunction to feeling. Fear acts as a vacuum that feeds secrecy and control. It works much like a bully on a playground. When everyone has fear of the bully, then the bully has power and is fed off this power. If however, transparency surfaces with those who have been bullied would come about, then the bully is suddenly reduced to a member of the community and is not exclusively separate. Transparency would then reveal that the bully has been using fear that has caused a lack of cohesiveness. When the group then gives up that fear, then the community becomes the strongest force. The bully can only be king as long as he is viewed as if he is on a throne. When the weakness of fear is revealed, then the higher energy momentum once again begins to progress and the transparency brings about empowerment.

Transparency is a practice that humanity needs to appreciate. This means that we will have to recognize our addiction to power, money, and control. It means that secrecy only serves to stunt our spiritual maturity. These lower energy momentums cannot allow the progression of humanity as a species. We must embrace transparency and allow our race to progress in a way that will bring about our realization that we are a race that is connected on every level regardless of the allocation of resources, understanding, money, power, and technology. Transparency is the next step in human spiritual evolution where we can achieve the appropriate use of free will.

Personal Responsibility

In our journey in life we seek many things. We try to fulfill our goals, obtain love, and achieve what we set as our own personal standards. However, there is a component that is essential to achieving spiritual maturity.

Personal responsibility is awareness that we are co creators in our lives and we choose to take the responsibility for our choices, actions, and reactions. We look beyond environment, circumstances, and individuals to discern appropriateness. We are aware that we have the power to react in situations. We have the power to create opportunities by our behavior and attitudes. We have to take personal responsibility for every aspect of our lives before we can truly mature.

Victim Mentality

Sometimes, dark things evade our lives and we find ourselves pushed to reveal parts of ourselves. We are on a journey to learn and grow in our circumstances and through this we will face certain obstacles that will either be our teacher or an opportunity to move on to something new in ourselves. If the path of teacher is warranted then we have a choice. We can choose the attitude of victim or we can allow ourselves to grow. This is a choice and we are the ones who decide. Some choose the victim role and this can improperly fulfill some emotional "needs". If one chooses to stay in the victim role for a period of time, then instead of personal growth, devaluation of the person can occur. We are always valuable, but we must be consciously aware in order to live it. When we are a victim then we are distracted by the victim traits and lose sight of the more meaningful aspects of ourselves.

Victim Path	The Spirit Chooses	Personal Responsibility
This is what happened to me	Creation from motive of thoughts	I am part of this and I choose to…
Focus is on oneself and the lacking	Formulation from Feelings	Focus is on seeking balance and stability of energy
Low energy momentum	Expression from generated emotion	High energy momentum
Action that reinforces belief or habits	Delivery of actions	Action reflecting balance

Victim Mentality/Personal Responsibility (Irene, Dianne 2009)

The bottom line is that the victim mentality is an indication that we are stuck on a lesson. The harshness of this reality is enough to keep some away from risks. Playing it safe will only mean that we remain still in our timeline of life. Because we live in the constraints of a three dimensional reality, we are always moving in a linear direction in our current awareness. This of course is an illusion as our spirit does not live in a linear constraint, but this serves as a plane where we can live a physical existence. Our choice will bring us success in that linear timeline or we will receive a failing grade and need to repeat that lesson.

Taking Responsibility

We are responsible for our thoughts. We are responsible for our feelings. We are responsible for our emotions. We are responsible for our actions. This means that we are responsible for finding the faulty breakdown between what we seek to create and what we act upon. Being consciously aware that we are responsible for our own journey and the reactions that we display on that journey, means that we alone are our biggest obstacle and our biggest asset.

Fear in Responsibility

Fear should never be the catalyst of a decision. While we will again acknowledged that the flight or fight mode can save a human from a chasing bear, most decisions in life are not based on that premise. Even if we do allow fear to bring us to a decision then we must also take responsibility for the consequences of that fear. When fear is in power then love is not being expressed. This means that we must do our best to come to terms with the fear in our lives.

Opportunities Created

When we do take responsibility and begin to be open enough to learn the lessons that are presented then we will begin to create opportunities. We will show that we have learned the lessons needed and the next steps can be explored. Our attitude will allow us to see the opportunities that are available. We also will be sending out positive reinforcement to our environment and preparing a way for positive circumstances. When negative situations or obstacles are present once more, we then need to behave in a way that shows we can move beyond that and see the lesson. Sometimes, we will also face circumstances for the benefit of others. Humanity is like a network and we are all connected. If we are to be used as a mirror or as a sounding board for others, then we must also consider this factor.

Being a Positive Force

When we are humble enough to see our part in the circumstances in our lives then we will become a positive force for ourselves and others who are also seeking to grow. Our personal responsibility creates a web that connects to the elements in our lives, but also the lives of others. We live in a dimension of free will where even our choice to be personally responsible is given. We should not take too long in deciding to be co-creators in the opportunities of our lives. To do so would mean that we would be stifled in the possibilities in our lives.

Guilt/Remorse

There is a vast difference between guilt and remorse. Guilt is a lower form feeling based out of the construct of shame in connection to consequences on us. It is an internalized process where the concern is for oneself. Remorse on the other hand is concerned with the effect our actions have had on others. It is energy that is concerned with the balance between others and us. The perspective is from the other to self. This is what allows for maturity and growing out of these "shame based" feelings. Remorse allows one to learn the perspective of others and how we affect them. When we are more concerned about how our actions affect the energy of others then we begin the Empathetic Process.

Expectations

Expectations are one of the biggest issues that lead to a broken link in communication and relationships. When we interact with others we tend to have a set of expectations. When these expectations are pure and of the spirit origin then the expectations are appropriate, but often in our modern society we have misconstrued expectations.

Inappropriate	Expectations	Appropriate
Expecting	Conscious and unconscious expectations	Appreciation
Dominance/ Submissiveness	⟺	Respect
Superficial happiness	⟺	Gratitude & Love
Control/ Emotional dominance	⟺	Trust

Expectations (Irene, Dianne 2009)

Practical Examples

Inappropriate		Appropriate
Expecting someone to make you happy	⟺	Taking responsibility for your own happiness
Expecting someone to make you feel a certain way: important, smart, powerful, etc.	⟺	Being grateful for gifts from others. Recognizing your insights, value, and traits.
Expecting others to see things your way	⟺	Learning to communicate in a way that others will find respectful even if they do not see things the way you do

Expectations Adapted (Irene, Dianne 2009)

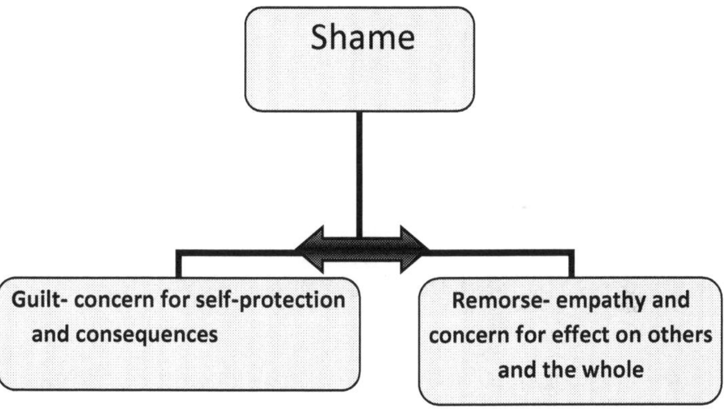

The Empathetic Process (Irene, Dianne 2009)

Empathy

I remember back as a child feeling things that I thought were a normal part of human sensing. When I would see an animal getting hurt, I would feel the pain from their perspective. When I would see another child get bullied, I would feel the pain of the child getting bullied. I would question how that bully could act that way and endure the pain they had caused on someone else. I had to realize that they could not feel what they had done. They were unaware and had to learn it for themselves. Some people do not have that innate ability to feel empathy. That means that some must be taught this very important truth of what they do to others.

We are creators and this creation begins with thought. Thoughts give birth to feelings. When this normal process is interrupted or a person lacks the ability to transfer their thoughts into the correct feelings, then empathy may not be part of this process. After having a near death experience when I was twenty, this truth was reinforced and I was reminded that we are all connected and everything we do has an effect on those around us. This means that we will all eventually see the lives we have lived as if we are in other's shoes.

The golden rule of treating others as we have been treated stems from the understanding that ultimately what we do contributes to a network of creation that connects to those around us. Ultimately, what we do to others is what we do to ourselves even if it is not fully realized until we leave this dimension.

Power Reaction

Some who do not have the correct development can develop a power reaction to this process. When they suppress or harm another, they generate a reaction to power. This process can set up a learned detriment. This process is not satisfying in itself and some will consume it like a drug. They can set out to experience it again seeking to satisfy the true missing component of empathy. This may not even be a conscious understanding to them.

As a result they will develop a pattern of thoughts that allows them to set themselves apart from others as entitled. Once this thought pattern is rooted, it can lead to feelings and then attitudes and actions that reinforce it. For some this can become an addiction cycle. This creates a place for these individuals to become potential power brokers rather than those who understand empowerment.

Predator Prey Mentality

This can further develop into a predator-prey mentality. A predator seeks out prey with one unconscious goal to generate power over their prey. This cycle does not go to the level of feeling with empathy. Instead, they become locked into a process that they can justify as a reality. They may incorrectly develop an understanding that others view the world as they do and in an attempt to not live out the weaker side of the prey and they will seek to be the predator more assuredly.

For some, this desire is developed as an unconscious perception of fear. These people develop a satisfaction generated on fear instead of an empathetic response that leads to a mature spiritual state. There is no doubt that Adolf Hitler followed such a process when he ordered sick children to be used in the testing of gas chambers. He was not capable of empathy or conceiving the pain that would be caused both physically and mentally to those who would be killed. Instead, he learned to feed his spirit by generating power over others that was generated by their fear.

Not only does this process generate a vacuum in the predator's spirit, but it also generates a vacuum that "steals" energy from their prey. Fear acts as a vacuum where love is absent. When love is present then our spirit and physical being are living in balance in this dimension and the dimension of the spirit.

Learning Empathy

It is essential for those who do not have an innate ability to feel empathy to learn this process even if they cannot truly feel what others feel. The acknowledgement of our actions as a direct reaction on others can still be a learned process that will enable an individual to progress to a more balanced state. Once they are aware that they are missing something, they may seek to understand and be open to what they may be missing. This realization will then offer an opportunity for them to evolve spiritually and be an active participant in their creation process that will bring about a positive directional growth for themselves and for those for which they interact.

Fear

Fear has plagued humanity for a very long time. Fear had its place in keeping Humans safe in case of danger, but our lives have become more sedentary and for most the danger we face is in our cars on busy streets. Fear was appropriate for those moments of need where our bodies would release extra adrenalin. Our minds switch from being in conscious thought to a mode of instinct. These instincts help to focus us on escaping immediate danger.

Most of the time, the manifestation of inappropriate fear occurs because we are not consciously functioning in the spiritual state. It manifests and serves as a defense mechanism to survive in a life threatening situation. When fear manifests in everyday life, it can cause a mismanaged spirit to devolve. Fear is a vacuum that creates a space for dissention and pain. It is a state that lacks love. Fear should be taken as a mechanism that keeps us from growing. Fear is like a vacuum for the spirit.

What happens when we stay in fear mode longer than a momentary state? Physically, adrenalin and cortisol can be released in continuous streams and can begin to wear on the body. This state which is meant for short periods is referred to as the fight or flight mode. What is happening mentally? We begin to focus on what are called lower order needs (Maslow,

1971). We focus our energy on safety and material needs. While we must take care of our basic needs, they should not be our primary focus and will cause stress.

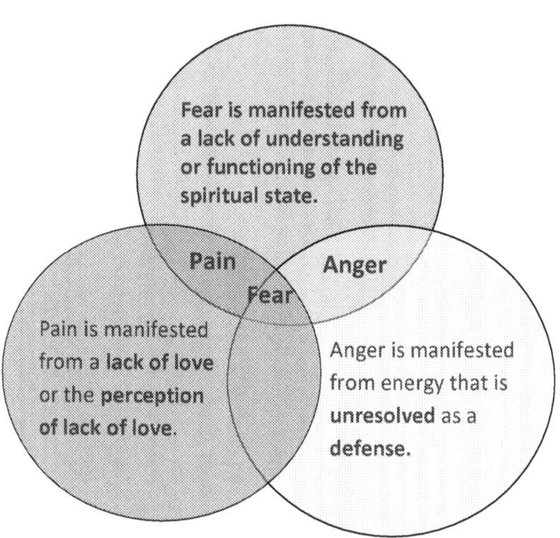

Pain/Fear/Anger Connection (Irene, Dianne 2009)

Fear Factor

Another consideration is the fear factor. Those who live in response to fear become a reactive component of reality. Their ability to be proactive is stifled and decisions are made on the basis of a lower plain of emotional intelligence. The extreme of this scenario can be seen in places where riots began or where wars began. Fear takes over the rational mind and forces a person to seek out what are considered to be the self preservation considerations. In this state growth and maturity are put on hold and self preservation uses up the senses. These senses are needed to continually register the nuances of reality and place them in the appropriate place in consciousness.

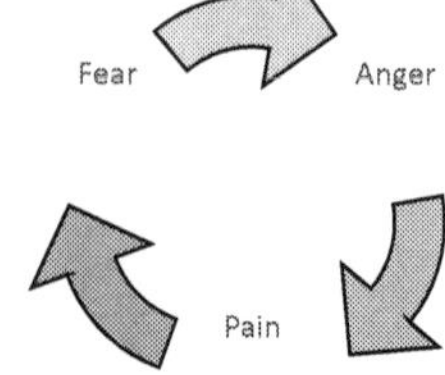

Fear Cycle (Irene, Dianne 2009)

The fear cycle plays a role in depression of the human spirit. This cycle creates a patterned habit which keeps one from growing. Fear and anger are related. When all fear is gone then anger will start to subside. Pain and fear are related. For example, a man who struggles with anger since childhood may be struggling with pain caused by his father's lack of love. If the father is absent or does not provide unconditional love, then a son can develop anger issues. This anger is really a coping strategy for covering the pain which grew his fears in life.

The Fear Level	Effect on Human Life
Fear becomes part of the everyday energy cycle.	The subconscious, the conscious, and the thinking cycle are shut down or slowed. This becomes a low form of existence. Fear acts as a vacuum and the focus of existence is to avoid pain, paranoia, and the false concept of loss of control. Looking at others in a negative manner possibly adopting the predator- prey mentality.
Fear sits at the driver's seat and is turned on or off at the conscious level.	The person functions at a mostly normal level on the surface, but when fear is triggered then the person becomes "helpless" to the fear.
Fear lives by a trigger standard.	Areas of a person's life are compartmentalized and activated when they are triggered.
Fear occurs only in times of danger	The only true purpose of fear in the human form. Fear beyond this level will only hinder the normal and progressive growth of a person's spirit.

The Fear Hierarchy (Irene, Dianne 2009)

Post Traumatic Stress

The problem of PSTD or Post Traumatic Stress is that they become stuck in the "fight or flight mode" which is a concept that was coined by Walter Bradford. The thinking is shut down and they can live in emotion and action or reaction where they are "safe" from the irrational thoughts or conflicting thoughts between their subconscious and consciousness.

Spirit- Subconscious Realm/Consciousness State
Thinking
Feeling
Emotions
Action/Reaction (Fight or Flight Mode)

Fight or Flight Mode Manifestation (Irene, Dianne 2004)

Emotions and Action/Reaction stages cause the person to be

unpredictable and appear to lack their original personality. Many who have been involved with war suffer from this because the reality of what they experienced has been too great of a shock to their consciousness. Deep in the human spirit beyond most of our human desires is an understanding of regret, remorse, and ultimately the need to be loved. War conflicts with this understanding in the subconscious and spirit of the individual. When the conscious interacts with this knowledge then the person is conflicted. The decision making process can be faulty and the person may function mostly at the emotion or action/reaction state. This would explain why they can revert by a simple stimulus. For example, a former service man may run and hide under a table when someone closes the door too loudly. The key is to get them to function at the top of the hierarchy. This will have to be done in steps and each level will need to be explored.

Power vs. Empowerment

How does power affect an individual? Those under a power thrive differently from those that are under empowerment. Power is concerned with control and empowerment is concerned with giving others power to contribute to an action or force.

"Power Bank Account"	
Power	**Empowerment**
Exercising power over others in the result of control	Exercising power to transfer power to others to encourage and ignite their own power for the advancement of the situation, personal growth, or group advancement.
Political rules designed to keep everyone in line.	Goals to set up an environment where individuals can contribute to tasks, environments, purposes, and outcomes.
Separation rules of groups designed to keep people in "boxes"	Working together as parts of the same body
Holding the power to create fear, harm, or end the life of another	Acknowledging that all are from the creator and have value, respecting each spirit as an individual expression which holds a connection to everyone else.

Power Bank Account (Irene, Dianne 2004)

War and Human Desire

There is unrest in the world and people are dying and lives are being cut short for a desire. After thousands of years, we still war amongst each other to find a solution and to express that desire. When will humanity learn to be good to each other? What causes people to resort to violence over a religion, political cause, a resource, or for vengeance? War is a primitive response to a desire of force. It creates chaos and causes human spirits to devolve on the personal and collective level.

Humanity has progressed substantially in technology over the last century. Our world has become a fast paced working machine. Resources are being gathered and used up at a faster rate than ever before. We are not living in balance of spirit, nature and technology. The population has greatly increased and wealth has been gathered into a smaller part of the population and continues to flow in that direction. Parts of the world are facing population decline while others are exploding. Change is a daily event. Our weather and atmosphere is in decline and selfishness and greed has begun to cause some governments to go bankrupt and be subject to the powerful.

The Solution

Whenever there are problems in any relationship we must look to the core of the human spirit. Greed, selfishness, hate, complacency, and a desire for power instead of empowerment, a lack of love, and kindness are always involved. No long drawn out story is needed. No conspiracy is needed. The reason is always related to those simple human conditions no matter what other details are present. We need to recognize this.

While up to this point our wars have been contained to a few countries, our technological advancements will allow us to war in a much greater way and over a much larger span. But why would we want to do this? Eventually, this warlike desire will lead to the destruction of our brothers and sisters. Not even the kind you were born with, but the ones on the other side of the planet that are part of your race: the human race. We all belong to each other and nothing we do is an island. We all have a trickledown effect on the entire human race.

There is no righteous reason to try to destroy another race, religion, group, or populous. Humanity is still very much like school children on a playground fighting over the basketball court. Our capacity for advancement spiritually has been abandoned to the advancement of technology and the greed for resources and power. Instead of recognizing that as a group we are only as great as our love and empowerment of others. The truth lies in that love and we will all see it from that perspective when we cross over into the next dimension. Many of us who have had that brush with death and returned can testify to this truth. Some leaders seek to treat their own people like cattle and hold all the resources for themselves. Some seek to create chaos to satisfy their fears and keep them from taking personal responsibility. Some sit idly by. Only when we see the travesty of this will we want to change. We all play a part in this. None of us are without shame as other humans are killed.

While people have a right to seek freedom, protection, and prosperity, there is also a human right of life and an opportunity to live out our purpose. The answer is not a strategic military strike, planned population reduction, or a victory in a battlefield. These can only serve to "defend" a people and put off the still true fact that the problem lies in the spirit of the human race. We need to solve our problems by growing and maturing our spirits. Imagine hypothetically, races from other planets observing our behavior. It would look so un-evolved to them. How can they destroy each other like this? We cannot trust them. They are not ready. Better yet, imagine the creator of the universe seeing what creation is doing to its own kind. We must learn to see this world from an outside perspective as we have gotten so narrowed by our technology and everyday lives.

Microscopy, Macroscopy, Ultrascopy

We have often taken a microscopic view of our world. It is easy to see things from our own perspective. Our small view of the world is perceived to be the center of reality. We forget that we are but a speck in the chain of galaxies and dimensions. The macroscopic view is seeing a much larger picture where we realize that we are this small part of a much larger picture. The macroscopic view would allow us to see from the outside perspective. The goal is to be able to see from all perspectives and adopt an Ultrascopy view of reality.

Microscopy	Macroscopy	Ultrascopy
Reality is seen from a single point of view. This creates a perspective that is focused on the small details of a single perspective.	Reality is seen from the view of the larger picture. This larger picture can give a top down perspective of reality.	Reality is viewed with considerations of every perspective on both the micro and macro perspective with an understanding of how elements are orchestrated.
For example: Human perspective.	For example: Perspective from another dimension	For example: Creator's perspective

Scopy Perspective (Irene, Dianne 2004)

We still need to strive for a better solution; a solution that leads to the growth of the human spirit. We should be caring for each other the way we want to be treated. It is such a simple concept, but one that can save humanity from the ultimate destruction and a neglected human spirit.

Chapter 3
OUR SPIRIT

Humanity has been created on this earth for several reasons. These reasons may not be completely in line with why our spirit is here. Our spirit is part of another dimension where the rules of reality are different than they are here in this realm. However, we are still connected to this realm and often desire more of its reality even if we are unaware of this. We travel to this dimension where we obtain a body that is formed inside of a chosen woman. When we are young we were more naturally ourselves until the environment we are in starts to provide a script for us to interact with. Society pulls and tugs at us and we learn to conform and react to the things around us. Hopefully, we become involved in a learning process where we will deviate from these environmental factors and can begin a process of spiritual growth.

Everything we experience here is "recorded" in our spirit even if our brain does not remember it. The body including the brain and the central nervous system is part of the organic mechanical body that we have to experience life this dimension. It is in no way the part that animates us. This is the spirit. There has been debate among some scientists as to the validity of the spirit. The purpose of this book is not to debate the existence of the spirit, but to provide you with an understanding of spiritual intelligence.

In other realms, creation works a little differently than it does here in the physical dimension. We can manifest instantly with our thoughts in the spiritual realm. In the physical realm, this process is not so easily achieved. However, the principle works the same. When we are in relationship to others, the creation process becomes dependent on the interaction and intent of both individuals. This is a beautiful design, but can also be heart breaking when two people are not creating together.

Pam Reynolds is one such case that can be used to help skeptics understand that science can in fact witness the spirit. This was the case when Pam had surgery for a brain aneurism where she was medically dead for about an hour. During that time she had an out of body experience and met spirits from the "other" side. When she was brought back to life and her brain resumed function, she was still able to recall what had happened outside of her body during that time that she was clinically dead. For those of us who have had a near death experience (NDE), we need no scientific proof, but we have come to know that indeed the spirit is very real and separate from the body. (Williams, 2002)

Near Death Experience

This question has been asked for centuries. Some have come to understand the time on this planet in our human body is a time to learn, grow, and love. Elizabeth Kubler Ross, a thantologist (one who studies death), studied more than 20,000 cases of NDE's (near death experiences) from those that had died and were brought back to life. She is one of the most respected authorities on the subject. As a psychiatrist, she began her studies from a more scientific perspective. As time went on, she became fully aware that death was a transition of life and not an end (Ross, 1991, 2008). Dr. Ross is well known for her stages of dealing with death. She has been an inspiration for hospice and her work continues to touch the lives of those dealing with loss.

Dr. Ross explains that there is a process to death. She states that it is the same for everyone despite your personal spiritual beliefs or culture. She compares it to a process of being born. After so many cases that she investigated, she no longer felt that faith was required to know that there was an "afterlife", but that she knew there was one. She desired to share this knowing with others.

She explains that there are three stages to dying. In the first stage she compares the body to a cocoon and the soul to a butterfly. She indicates that the body is damaged or no longer functions. She compares it to moving from a home to a more wonderful home. The second stage is where you will leave this cocoon and you are transformed in the spiritual sense. She describes it as being provided with "psychic energy". In the second stage when your soul has left your body, you come to the realization of what is happening at your place of death. She explains that it is beyond human consciousness. In the third stage, a life review will take place. You will become aware of the fact that time and space does not have the constraints that it once did. It should be noted that at the time of the review you will indeed see your life along with the perspective of everyone that you have touched and interacted with. You will know their perspective as well.

NDE of Three

The labels that we have used in our human culture are not necessary in the afterlife. Individuals experience various presences in their NDE's because the other dimension is much more spiritually developed than the physical realm. Those that are Christian will see figures in the form that is of comfort to them. Those that are Buddhist will see the figures that bring them comfort. Upon researching thousands of NDE stories, it becomes clear that this is the case. One such example involves three people of different religions that shared a near death experience when they were struck by lightning (Hoyer, 2000).

During the fall of 1971, when I was 22 years old, I shared a near-death experience with my cousin, James, and his best friend, Rashad, who was from India. Both young men were on a break from school and were staying with my family on our farm. One afternoon the three of us went to the cornfield to cut fodder. To get to the field we had to go through a metal gate, and we took turns climbing down to open and shut it. By late afternoon a storm started brewing in the west, and we decided to quit for the day. It was James' turn to open the gate, and as he did so, he reached up for my arm to climb back up onto the wagon. I was leaning the wrong way, and his weight pulled me toward him. Rashad grabbed my other arm to steady me and we were in just this position when the lightening hit us.

I saw the lightning sparkle along the top of the gate. The next thing we knew, we were in a large room or hall made of dark stone. The ceiling was so high and the gloom was so thick we couldn't see the top. There were no furnishings or wall hangings, just cold, black stone all around. I knew I should be afraid, but I just felt peaceful, floating along there in the gloom with my two friends in the great, dark hall. The stately walls of this place loomed above us and seemed to radiate both great power and also great masculinity. I remember thinking it would have suited King Arthur. It was at that point that I realized that the three of us were united in thought and body. Images of Arthur came to me from James and Rashad. James saw only a cosmic version of the king. Rashad seemed to [be] envisioning himself in the time of Arthur. As we all became conscious of each other's thoughts, I suddenly knew James and Rashad better than I have ever known anyone else.

We realized there was light coming into the chamber from an archway at one end. It was more than just light. It was a golden, embracing warmth. It gave off a feeling of peace and contentment more intense than anything we had ever felt. We were drawn toward it. We weren't talking, but we were communicating with each other on some other level, seeing through each other's eyes. As we came to the archway and passed through, we entered a beautiful valley. There were meadows and tree-lined hills that led to tall mountains in the distance. Everything glistened with golden sparks of light.

We saw that the sparkling lights were tiny, transparent bubbles that drifted in the air and sparkled on the grass. We realized that each tiny sparkle was a soul. To me, the valley appeared to be Heaven, but at the same time I knew that James and Rashad were seeing it differently. James saw it as the Gulf of Souls. Rashad saw it as Nirvana, and somehow we knew all this without speaking. The light began gathering at the far end of the valley, and slowly, out of the mist, a pure white being began to materialize. I saw an angel with a strong, bright face, but not like you'd usually imagine. She was closer to a strong, Viking Valkyrie. I knew she was the special angel that watches over the women of my family, and I perceived her name to be Hellena. James saw this same being as his late father, a career Naval officer, in a white dress uniform. Rashad perceived the being to be the Enlightened One, or Buddha.

The being spoke first to Rashad and welcomed him. He said that Rashad's time on Earth was done. He was worthy now of Nirvana. Rashad asked why James and I were there and was told that we were part of the reason why he was worthy of Nirvana. His two great friends loved him so much that they had willingly accompanied him on his last journey. At the same time, however, James received a different message. He had been worried about what his father would think about his anti-war protest activities, and his father told him he was proud of him for standing up for what he believed. He knew he was not a coward because a coward would not have made this journey with Rashad. I received yet another message in which Hellena told me she was glad I had remembered the example of strength, honesty, wisdom, and loyalty taught to me by my family.

We spent what seemed like an eternity in this place as we talked to our separate, yet joined, entities. They said they appeared to us in this way because back in the real world we were physically joined when the lightning struck us. They said it also symbolized the joining of all religions and doctrines. They said I would live to see a new age of tolerance, that the souls and hearts of humanity would be joined as the three of us were.

The guides taught us that doctrine and creed and race meant nothing. No matter what we believed we were all children joined under one God, and that the only rule was God's true law - do unto others as you would have them do unto you. We should treat all people as if they were a part of our soul because they were. All living things in the universe were connected to one another. They said that soon humanity would mature enough to assume a higher place in the universal scheme of things, but until then we must learn acceptance and tolerance and love for each other. They said there would come a new age when people would not be able to endure seeing others homeless and hungry. We would realize that only by helping each other could we truly help ourselves.

Eventually we were told that it was time to go. We would not be allowed to stay longer because it was not yet time for me or for James, only for Rashad. The enlightened one told Rashad he would have a little time before he returned to take care of his worldly affairs. James' father told him he would return to this place soon after Rashad, but the two of them had to go back for now so that I could. I said I would willing stay here in this valley with them, but Hellena told me that I had not fulfilled my destiny; that I had children yet unborn.

We drifted slowly toward the archway. The pull became stronger and we were literally thrown back into the world. We floated for a while there, hovering above our bodies. Some of my cousins had been in the next field and had seen what had happened. We saw them all come running to where we lay. James and Rashad's hands were still stuck to my arms. We saw my cousins pry their fingers loose so they could turn Rashad over to help him.

When our hands were pried loose, James and I re-entered our bodies. We felt as if we were on fire, but it turned out that we had only minor injuries. Rashad, it seemed, being on the end, had taken most of the charge. The doctors said that the lightning had caused damage to his heart, lungs, and liver. He remained in the hospital for several weeks. During that time, tests revealed that James had a brain tumor that would eventually claim his life.

As soon as Rashad could travel, James took him home to India. He offered to stay, but Rashad told him that he wished solitude for his final time. Rashad took on the life of the Ascetic, in the Vedic tradition. He asked his wife to stay with her family because he wanted his last days to be spent in spiritual awakenings. About a year and a half later, on a cold day in January, Rashad returned to Nirvana. James and I knew when his soul left the world without being told.

James lived about three years after he found out he had the brain tumor. He gave most of his considerable inheritance to a charity that educated young people in India. I, on the other hand, have survived for another thirty years (so far) with the knowledge that this experience which I shared with my closest friends has been a guiding force in my life. I strive every day to meet my destiny, whatever it may be, with the same quiet dignity and resolution they showed when they met theirs. They have truly been my pathfinders, and I know that the connection I shared with them so long ago is the same connection we all share. We just sometimes fail to realize it.

Carl Jung

Psychiatrist, Carl G. Jung, who has been credited as one of the fathers of psychology with his research in the area of personality testing and other concepts also experienced a near death experience after suffering from a heart attack. In his autobiography, *Memories, Dreams, Reflections* Jung describes hovering above the earth and approaching a floating structure that resembled a temple.

He stated that it began with a process of shedding. This involved his emotions, thoughts, and every part of himself. He states that it was quite painful. After this shedding, he had an awareness of everything that happened in his life from multiple perspectives. He seems to indicate that he was experiencing what has been described by many other that have had a NDE where you understand life and its connections to everyone and everything else. He stated that he was a combination of, "what has been" and "what has been accomplished." This realization brought about humility and a sense of wholeness. He was at peace and understood his existence. He could see his existence from a more objective perspective. This is a common transition for those that experience a stage of death.

At this point his spirit left the earth and he was hovering far above the earth and began to focus on a temple in space. He had a sense of being at home and knowing the people inside the temple. He felt a sense of understanding of how he fit into the history of his own soul. He found that his existence fit into a cycle of time and that he existed outside of time. He was anticipating entering the temple. Then he saw what he calls a primal state of his doctor and the image of the doctor said that there was an agreement that he should not leave the earth.

It was decided that he would return to earth and Jung was disappointed by this decision. He did in fact return and spent some time trying to overcome that disappointment. He had changed and suddenly realized that his spirit was very separate from his body. This changed Jung and his perspective of the world was changed.

It was several weeks before he felt as if he was really living again in the earthly realm. He didn't eat and watched the mountains from his bed. He felt as if they were just curtains with holes like a used newspaper. He could not find meaning in them. He felt as if he had returned to a "box system". Jung had seen behind the curtain in the play of life and he would never be the same. He felt as if the physical world we have was artificial and that he had to convince himself to resume life. He compared his feelings to being in prison and he was glad that he had moved on from being "hung up in a box by a thread". Perhaps, because of the transition through the veil, Jung was able to see his doctor in spirit as well. He knew that his doctor was sick and told him that, but the doctor did not want to hear it. Shortly after, the doctor died.

There can be little doubt that such an experience would influence his writings in psychology. He held the belief that the human spirit was the foundation of life (Hollis, 2008). He indeed did have a mission to complete. His work laid the foundation for all personality testing in the field of psychology and did a great deal to help humans understand how this affects their lives. Today his teachings appear in textbooks across the world and he is noted as one of the father's of modern psychology.

The unconscious psyche believes in life after death

– Carl Jung, MD

Chapter 4
7 UNIVERSAL TRUTHS

The next dimension does not need religion to exist. Religion is manmade. The spirit is not manmade. This means that we all take different paths and learn different things according to our perspectives in our life which provides a culture and environment. In the next dimension, there are universal truths that surpass any religion. Some of these universal truths are as follows:

1. All life is sacred.
2. We are all part of each other and there are many types of beings that are on their own paths of discovery.
3. What we experience here is part of our journey to learn, grow, and love
4. We are eternal beings.
5. Unconditional love is the ultimate state of life and our purpose in life is to ultimately become love.
6. There are universal laws of the dimensions set in place by the Creator.
7. We are co-creators in life.

Dimensional Truths

1. **ALL LIFE IS SACRED**

All life that has been animated has value. Even down to the smallest form, it is part of life that originated from the source. Each one has come here to be part of this dimension in some way. Each human being has come here from another dimension to experience life. We should be mindful of this as we interact with others. Every interaction we have with others is recorded in the spirit. This means that when we go to the next dimension we will review our lives and see it from more than one perspective because the spirit transcends the physical limitations. We will view our interactions from the other person's perspectives. Every action and reaction has more than one perspective. You will experience that in the spirit and know it as you know your perspective now. Those who are more spiritually mature are aware of this and have been shown to be those who wish to contribute to humanity.

Mother Teresa is an example of someone who understood that perspective was selective. She became a fully fledged nun at about 28 years old. She felt another perspective when she walked past a needy person. She did not see it from her perspective, but felt what they felt. This perspective caused her to be the most well known nun on the planet. She won a Nobel Peace Prize in 1979 (Nobel Lectures, Peace, 1971-1980). She was open to experiencing this. We must be open to experiencing our "awakening experience" in order to benefit from it.

What about Animals?

Animals have also come here to experience life. We should be mindful of this as we interact with them. Animals have a spirit. Thousands of NDE experiencers will testify to the realization that the spirits of animals exist in the next dimension. They are capable of pain, suffering, love, excitement, comfort, fear, and joy. Some animals are even sensitive to the other dimensions in ways that we often miss. Any animal that we abuse will also be included in our review of life and we will understand that experience from their perspective. This is perfect justice. This is judgment. It is fair.

The mass killing of animals that takes place on this planet today is in fact a reality that these animals feel. We have gotten away from cohabitation in a balanced way upon this planet. Manipulation of the balance of life has led to much unneeded suffering by the animals that have come here to be our companions and to experience their own journey. I realized that many reading this will have difficulty with these words, but they are the truth and once we are aware of this, we are changed. The UN Food and Agriculture Organization estimate that over 58 billion animals are terminated for food purposes alone in the world in 2008. The methods of handling, caging, and slaughtering these animals is an eye opening and shocking realization.

No one can decide for you that you should be vegan or vegetarian, but the understanding of the spiritual aspect of partaking in an animal industry is part of understanding. This understanding is an awareness of how our actions as humans have an effect upon others. There are several factors that need to be understood as part of the bigger picture.

1. The hunting process of predatory animals like a lion play out like this: The lion sees an animal move and his instincts become heightened. He salivates and desires to rip through their flesh. He is not affected by the screams of the animal as it fights for its life. Instead, he leaps for the kill. He

subdues the animal until it dies. Then he begins dismantling its body piece by piece. Blood is everywhere and organs are exposed. The flesh is raw and he rips it in pieces.

Most humans would find this distasteful. Most humans do not follow this scenario in their own lives. Humans do not salivate at the sight of a deer or cow. Humans do not wish to bite into their flesh raw and rip them apart. In fact, if most humans had to hunt for their food, they simply would not do it. Instead, we wrap cuts of animal flesh that have been enhanced with chemicals like formaldehyde to make them look appealing. Then they are cooked and consumed with a fork and a knife. Most live nutrients are no longer part of the picture. Humans have found a way to make it look more civilized, but someone had to kill that animal in order to get it to your plate and you did not have to see this animal fight for its life, show fear and pain as it was sliced or shot. It is a violent process.

2. Humans are the only beings that must cook their animal flesh before eating it. Animals that do consume other animal flesh do so when it is fresh and the nutrients are still "alive" and beneficial to the animal. Their intestines are shaped like a garden hose. This allows what could be harmful things like bones and other parts to pass safely from their system. The human digestive tract is different from this. Human intestines are wavy and match those that eat vegetation. They also have fangs while humans have teeth of a vegetarian.

3. The physical state of the animal is affected by their emotional state. When someone is angry, a signal is sent out telling the rest of their cells that they are angry. The same is true of fear. This message is then translated to the flesh that humans consume. Large amounts of adrenalin and information in the DNA that tells a story to your DNA even if you are not thinking of it. This means that the fear, pain, and anger that the animal feels in the moments before death are now coded into the flesh that is consumed. In fact, some slaughter houses have become aware of this and decided that the adrenalin rush changed the flavor of the soft tissue and have begun killing some animals in horrific ways such as throwing them in vats of boiling oil. The animal dies a horrifying death. What they may not understand is that that information is stored in the DNA that humans are consuming. It is encouraged that you do some research on reports of those that have had blood transfusions and how they noticed a change in themselves after doing so. It is possible that this information can be understood at the cellular level.

4. The mass production of animal flesh for consumption has led to a harsh and disgusting environment for the animals. These animals die under extreme conditions and this has an effect on their life experience in this lifetime. It is animal abuse and it is suggested that you conduct your own research on this matter. A good place to start is a book called, *Slaughter House.* Animals are on their own journey and have come to experience life. When one looks into the eyes of animals, remember that they have a spirit just like us. Remember that they were also given life. Some animals have even come with a mission for humans. Some have inspired humans, saved humans, and even served as teachers.

Oscar

There is a cat named, Oscar, who lives in a nursing home. He has a special sense. He has a form of spiritual intelligence. He knows when someone is going to die. He is able to sense who will die next and sits with them shortly before they pass on. The staff became believers after many visits with the residence in which they observed an uncanny accuracy for who would die next. He was so accurate that he could visit within minutes of a patient's passing. Even patients that showed no sign of soon passing would get visits from Oscar if it was their time to go. In a book entitled, *Making Rounds with Oscar*, David Dosa, M.D. describes Oscar's ability to sense the right time. One particular patient named Ralph seemed to be close to death and the staff was making him comfortable. When they placed Oscar down, he protested and left. About 36 hours later, Oscar began to pace in front of Ralph's door. When Oscar was let in the room, he lay close to Ralph and stayed until the funeral director attended Ralph.

Science has also come to realize that interaction with animals is one of the best stress relievers. It appears that the unconditional love that they so freely display is food for our spirit. We know that dolphins can use their senses to understand an injury to the human body. They also feel empathy for swimmers that are drowning and have rescued them many times. They are also capable of deviant behavior if trained to participate in it. Both of these are also human traits that we are capable of displaying. Yet, we are slaughtering dolphins in droves in Japan as if they are merely an object for our use. These animals are highly intelligent and are able to communicate to other dolphins to describe their pain and fear as they are being slaughtered. These fishermen will feel the slaughter of the dolphins when they cross over to the other side from the dolphin's perspective. In other words, in the full spiritual state, they will experience the empathy that they were lacking while on this physical plane.

2. ALL IS ON A PATH OF DISCOVERY.

We are all part of each other and there are many types of beings that are on their own paths of discovery. Each person or living thing here has come by divine placement. In other words, there is a system of entrance into this dimension. We are all part of this process. We are all also part of a bigger process beyond the cycle of a lifetime on this planet. Dimensional reality is still a difficult thing for many to grasp. However, science is beginning to see glimpses beyond the veil. The human life we live on this planet is a small part of the bigger picture.

In other dimensions there are other beings that exist. We are clearly not the most evolved race and exploring ancient texts reveals a pattern of discussions of other beings. The Sumerian texts have a creation story much like the Bible and other ancient texts. What they have in common is that they all indicate other realms with other beings. In modern times, we have had colonels, astronauts, and others report experiences as well. In olden times we had names for these experiences. They were identified as monsters, demons, and angels. Then aliens and inter-dimensional beings were also identified. Their labels are really irrelevant. All living things give off a form of energy. What matters more is that we learn to discern energy as negative and positive.

The Veil

When a human body dies the energy in this dimension will begin to drop in frequency until the body is no longer functional. As the energy is drained in connection to the body, then it makes the transition into the veil. This veil is like a curtain between dimensions. This may explain the reoccurring stories of a tunnel in NDE's. When someone is on the cusp of the veil, they can also experience communication or can see a family member that is deceased. Stories have been shared with family members a short time before their passing talking about a relative coming to see them and telling them that it will be alright or giving them some other message. As the spirit makes its transfer to the next dimension, the window opens and some seem to have one "foot" here and one in the veil.

When my Aunt Linda was dying she experienced a NDE before leaving permanently. Her mother, my grandmother came to her and told her that it would be alright. Then she told her that she had a message for others. Each of these messages was specific and meaningful to just them. It had an impact on my uncle at the time and gave him hope of what was on the "other side".

The veil may be the link discussed in the string theory. Smaller than atoms, neutrons or electrons, strings may be the physical connection at the micro level between the physical and the dimensional realms. The elements that make up the smallest components of the atom are vibrating strings. These strings are then how matter manifests itself in the physical realm. When these strings become unattached to the veil (brane) and become circularly attached to themselves then they become open to transfer through other dimensions beyond the veil. Scientists have speculated that there are multiple dimensions and strings manifest into numerous dimensions. Beyond that, scientists have suggested that in the higher dimensions that strings are different and manifest more as a membrane (R. Kayne, 2011). Perhaps this correlates to the idea that the higher dimensions no longer need to manifest in the physical sense. If we are indeed on what is considered the third dimension, then the higher (less dense) one goes on the dimensional levels then the physical becomes less required.

What part of us goes on?

Our spirit is the true part of ourselves. Thoughts are the judgments we make in our reflection of the environment and ourselves. Emotions are merely expressions that manifest as a result of our feelings. These feelings are born from our thoughts or the lack of correct thought. Fear is a vacuum where our energy actually changes and we move away from love. Fear is not part of us in the next dimension. Pain is not part of us in the next dimension. While we will review these things in our review of life, they will not be a permanent part of our spirit. We will be aware of them as an outside existence of our spirit. They are something that our spirit experiences, but they do not originate from our spirit. Our spirit will exist with the positive energies of love and peace. The negative energies will be sloughed away when we go into a dimension of higher vibration.

All of the experiences we have had are part of the creation that our spirit has interacted with. We take our experiences with us. Our spirit will leave our body and we will realize how big our spirit is compared to the body that we use to experience this physical realm. During my NDE, I became all too aware of how tiny my body was and wondered how my spirit could have fit. I pondered on that point for some time afterwards. I saw my body as a mechanical shell that was so much heavier than the spirit. That realization if very freeing and the connection with the creator is truly realized.

Why do some have dark NDE's?

The next dimension and the dimensions beyond that are expansive. The rules of dimension are different than they are here in our realm. Someday science may come to discuss dimensions within dimensions. While most near death experiences are pleasant, there are those who experience something very dark. Imagine an attempt to commit suicide. You suddenly go to a dimension that was dark and scary. You could see creatures preparing you for something and they doing things to you. They leave your side and suddenly you sense someone and can hear someone breathing. You feel their presence is pure evil. (Could we say a lack of love?) You have been transported where creatures exist that are not on the same spiritual journey that you were meant to be on.

Some religions call this hell, but it is a dimension just as our world is a dimension. Those who go there may have some energy level that draws their spirit there as they are passing through the veil between dimensions. You can visualize this as a room in a building. If we get lost, we may enter the wrong room. Our spirits were not created to go to this place, but it does exist. This is just one of many dimensions and we have only begun to realize the reality of dimensions in quantum physics. Most NDE experiencers report that when they call out for help- "think" that they do not wish to be there, then they are pulled elsewhere. Some report that when they realize that they are being toyed with or fooled, they have the ability to leave. This dimension has a low energy level. It feels like pure "evil" or what we can call a very low energy level. Our spirits are designed to exist in a higher dimension. That is why fear or a vacuum takes hold when they experience this. In choosing love and rejecting the fear and evil, they are often able to move on.

Lower Dimensions	Physical Dimension	Higher Dimensions
Negative NDE's	Our current existence	Positive NDE's

Dimensions (Irene, Dianne 2012)

Some people decide to be born into favorable conditions and some people decide to be born into unfavorable conditions. The choice has to do with satisfying divine justice and karma.
Edgar Cayce

3. LIFE IS A JOURNEY TO LEARN, GROW, AND LOVE.

What we experience here is part of our journey to learn, grow, and love. Imagine if an ethics class was part of the educational system just as math or science currently is a part of the system. Perhaps, we would value the spiritual development as a human race much more than we currently do. The truth is that we spend very little time or effort in our spiritual development compared to where we spend the rest of our efforts. Beyond religious training, we should be seeking to understand ourselves, others, and our world. We should be schooled on how to pick a spouse, or how to develop your strengths and abilities beyond a text book. Most of these areas become peripheral venues beyond our main stream life. Because of this, we are forced to learn many things the hard way. Thankfully, the other side is well aware of this and our progress can still be found. However, our progress is much slower than it could be. That is why the emphasis on spiritual intelligence is so important.

Love

The highest asset in this lifetime is having a person in your life that loves you, trusts you, and cherishes you. They are better than a 60 billion dollar deal. They are food for your spirit. However, some will not realize this if they are not open and unwilling to grow. Many of us are encouraged with everyday life to live a very physical life. We pursue riches and power, but those things are fleeting and the oppressive energy that it can create will also be part of our review when we cross over.

We all have lessons to learn. Some have come to teach as well. A child with Down's syndrome is a good example. These children see the world from a specific perspective. They are capable of love and may remind us what is really important. Some mothers have reported that these children often teach them about spiritual qualities in their own lives. These children have spirits living inside their bodies that are just like the rest of us. They have full mental abilities when they cross over to next dimension. There they are whole and perfect.

Many NDE's will report that they come to understand our purpose in this life. They are met with figures that instruct them on why they must return. They will be told that they still have unfinished business, love to give or receive, lessons to learn, and tasks to complete. There are specific purposes for our stay here in this timeline and we have come to fulfill them. We do have free will and so our journey will be one of possibilities and opportunities. It is very possible that young children who die are here to fulfill a specific purpose and then are released from life.

Learn and Grow

Some have come to influence others or be part of their lives. Most will find this not as an exclusive mission, but a complementary one. It is possible for two spirits to be strategically placed so that they are more likely to interact. It is also realistic that we are born unto specific parents who will provide a certain environment for our learning. However, our free will becomes a place where we make choices about what we will do with our lives and how we will treat others.

4. WE ARE ETERNAL BEINGS

Imagine standing in line and speaking to a person who says it is time now. You speak about life and this person says there are things that you still need to deal with, experience, or learn. Suddenly you are whisked away like a vapor of light and you leap into your mother's womb. There you begin to form and experience your first physical sensation in this lifetime. You are born, grow and experience life with no memory of what came before your experience in the womb. However, you did exist before you were put into a human body. Most of us cannot remember that part of our existence. When this physical form no longer functions, we will return to that place where we will review our lives, rest, gain insight, and continue to live.

5. UNCONDITIONAL LOVE IS ONE'S GREATEST ACHIEVEMENT.

Unconditional love is the ultimate state of life and our purpose in life is to ultimately become love. We must learn and come to understand love and loving others, and then we will probably not return to earth unless we have another mission. Our goal of living in this life time is to evolve our spirit and the spirits of others. The hierarchy of existence is an unending expanse that humans have yet to fully grasp in this existence.

Many people throughout history have desired to achieve great things. Some have desired to conquer lands and people. Some have desired to achieve a title or status in society. While others have desired fame or a glory associated with some task. These things have filled many of the days for some lifetimes. For some at the end of their story, they may have declared their satisfaction with experiencing what few have had. However, a human's ultimate arrival in life is something that is not associated with these achievements.

It all comes down to a foundation of one journey no matter the details. The greatest journey for every human spirit is the journey of love. Whether this love is between two people, for orphans, or to live a life of service to progress some aspect of human life, it still is about love. Some greats of history have sought this great service to humanity and thus been unable to cherish the aspects of personal relationship with a mate, but still they contributed greatly with great love for humanity, while others have made use of everyday love in kindness, effort, or discovery.

Still some seek to leave a legacy of good will to humanity such as those who have lived rather solitary lives. These individuals have been considered rare. Some of these greats have been a kin to Mother Teresa. One such great was blessed to have lived among the normal path of family and love such as Gandhi. While some others have been like them, but did not receive the recognition, because they were extraordinarily different. For example, Tesla was a great man who never married and lived a very solitary life. He had great contributions to give to humanity including x-ray, infrared, radio, the peace ray, and more than 80 trunks full of scientific ideas found after his death. Regardless of humanity lacking care in how they spent the knowledge gained, Tesla gave great things to humanity. These greats often live a life that few have strove for in current times of human history. Society has offered too much distraction for the majority to seek such lives, and others have been meant for different journeys. Those individuals not meant to be a Mother Teresa can still reach a purpose in love.

The key is ultimately for us to become unconditional love. This means that the societies that separate us are merely obstacles in our way of growing up as a species. We live these lives with different paths that all lead to the same place. This place is where we must think, choose, and grow. Those who have given into greed, power, and entitlement have missed the mark of our journey and only act as an obstacle in our progression. Each sacred life upon this planet is all part of the same circle. The most real part of us is not of flesh, but of spirit which is only on borrowed time here.

This school called life is a stage for all of us to act out our purpose and to become more than when we came. Some play out their lives as if they know the script and some get lost in the props upon the stage and do not really get into their performance. Others remain reactionary and others seek to steal plots that do not belong to them. Still we are all part of the same cycle. We have come to be students of time and spirits in flesh with the purpose of becoming unconditional love.

6. THERE ARE UNIVERSAL LAWS OF THE DIMENSIONS

Many people are familiar with the laws of thermodynamics. For example, the first law states that energy is changed from one form to another, but it is not destroyed. These laws were defined to understand how the forces of the physical realm work and interact with other forces and elements. This concept can also be applied to the spiritual realm. For instance, once a person reaches a certain progression on the other side during a NDE, they will be unable to come back to their physical body. Many experiencers attest to that understanding. Some are not allowed to enter past a gate or threshold.

The connection of our body and our spirit is multi-dimensional. Our body acts as a vehicle to house our spirit. It is much like putting on virtual reality gear and playing a game. The difference is that the universe's system is so sophisticated that many forget that we are not our physical selves.

7. WE ARE CO- CREATORS IN LIFE

The Creator is experiencing the universe through us. We are learning to experience the world through a growing process that allows us to experience life in a physical way. The physical realm allows us to experience the aspects of life as confined to this realm. This realm offers a place to manifest our thoughts into our feelings and emotions as an interaction of physicality. We have a chance to progress our spirits in this physical realm. We interact, create, and use circumstances to grow and learn to love.

Chapter 5
SPIRITUAL BANK ACCOUNT

The Spiritual bank account concept works well to take inventory of how to balance the inputs and outputs of your life. It is a tool to work through depression and to reflect on personal growth. It works much like a traditional bank account where a balance should exist in the positive in order to create positive emotional health. An account that cancels out to zero is not a place of growth. The idea is to have a positive amount in your bank account. Everyone will find that each withdrawal and deposit will hold a different value and must be matched with an equivalent value in order to find balance. Once the withdrawal and deposits are written in the columns it is then important to go back and find the "Emotional and Feeling" value of each one. These values are a reflection of what is brought forth by the thought value of each experience. This value is the key to recognizing our desires and needs. Each withdrawal or deposit can be written in greater detail than the sample below. The more detail the input, the more likely the value can be identified.

Negative Withdrawal		**Positive Deposit**	
Circumstance or Event	Value	Circumstance or Event	Value
Divorce/ Break up	Rejection, pain, separation from love, sadness, depression, loneliness	Meditation/ Prayer	Peace, comfort
Death	Sadness, separation, loneliness	Support Group	Emotional support, positive influence
Job Loss	Frustration, financial stress	Spending time with friends	Emotional support, positive influence
Financial Problems	Negative stress, worry, self-worth issues	Hobbies	Stress outlet, balance
		Counseling	Thought reflection

Negative/Positive-Withdrawal/Deposit Slip (Irene, Dianne 2004)

Here is an example of how to use the spiritual bank account for a personal account. The subject name: Sam. Current situation: Recently divorced, wife cheated, lost custody, laid off from work, facing depression, anxiety, and loss of interest in life.

Sam's Spiritual Bank Account	
Negative Withdrawal	Positive Deposit
Divorce- rejection, failure, questioning purpose and identity (10)	**Support group**- support, understanding personal conflict, outlet, comfort, reassurance. (5)
Ex-wife cheated- betrayal, self worth questioning, trust issues, anger (9)	**Friends**- building trust, support, acceptance, stress relief (5)
Laid off of work- defeated, identity crisis, stress, financial focus, frustration (7)	**New work /education**- change of environment, sense of hope, identity defining, part of a group (7)
Shared custody of children- pain, sadness, despair (9)	**Quality Time**- influencing children in a positive manner, identity building, sense of worth (5)
	Hobbies- release of frustration and stress (3)
	Meditation- release of frustration, stress, and nurture (3)
Total: 35	Total: 28

Spiritual Bank Account (Irene, Dianne 2004)

It is important that the positive deposit be more than the negative withdrawal. In other words, the account should not equal zero or even out. The healthy spiritual bank account should always be in the positive with the deposits being more than the negative withdrawals otherwise; the person will be merely surviving. Once the withdrawals and deposits are analyzed, a number value can be given to each factor. This can assist with balancing the spiritual bank account. In the example above, Sam still has some work to do even though it looks as though his spiritual bank account is in the positive. He needs to continue to deposit values in order to come out in the positive. Only then will he be thriving.

THE BOX

The Box is an exercise in letting go of the things that do not need to be carried or burdened upon our spirits. We build up negative energies, stress, guilt, sorrow, anger, and sadness that are not meant to be a permanent part of our spirit. There are two versions of the exercise. You can try both to find the one that works best for you. The idea is to be comfortable in this process and some may need more practice than others.

1. It should begin with all distractions begin removed from your environment. Some find it easiest to try this lying down and done before bed.

2. The process of relaxing all parts of the body beginning with the feet and moving up to the head should be completed before mentally entering the room.

3. The process should be done with several deep breaths before the relaxation begins. Start with your feet and cover every major body part until you reach your head. Once you feel that you cannot be distracted, focus on your breathing until you are comfortable in the room with the box.

4. Some participants have reported that the white room is too intense for them. In this case, the garden version will work best. Just as individuals report seeing various things when they cross over, everyone's mind is unique.

Garden Version

Imagine that you are in a garden. This garden is quiet and peaceful. There is a large bolder in the center of the garden and upon this boulder is a box. There is a light that glows from inside the box. You approach the box and stand in front of the box. Your body is covered in black ink blots. These ink blots are your troubles. You bring them with you to have them removed and go into the box. These ink blots easily are released from your clothes and skin. They will go easily into the box. You can remain there as long as you need to in order to remove the inkblot stains. Once they are in the box they cannot come out and they take with them the energy of that event, time, or feeling. This exercise will allow the release of hidden as well as obvious issues. It may take multiple tries before you are relaxed enough to let go and this should not be seen as a failure. There are different emotional strengths to each factor in your life. Some will require more work than others.

White Room

Imagine that you are in a white room. The walls are white and the floors are white. The ceiling is also white. You are dressed in white. The table in the center of the room is white. The box has no lid and there is a light that glows from inside the box. Once you are fully focused on the room, you will begin to use the box to take in your negative energies. These energies can come from left over negative experiences and difficulties that you have had in your life. These things can be resolved or unresolved, but they are left over pieces of emotion and feeling that you are still attached to. These things appear as black ink blots. They will suddenly appear on you, the walls, or ceiling. They can appear anywhere in that room. You will begin to visualize these ink blots floating into the box. Once they are inside the box, you will be released from their hold, their karma, their pain, control, and their power. You can stay in this room for as long as you need to, but it is not necessary to get rid of all the issues at one time. It is also ok to leave the room with some of the ink blots still present. You can return and deal with them once again. The purpose of the white contrast is to separate the black energy of the lower energy sources in your life with that of the white or higher energy sources in your life. When you have mastered this visualization, your feelings will come much easier in relation to the release of these things into the box. Once they enter the box, they are released into the universe and no longer are part of your environment. They are going back to the source to be transformed into something more useful, but you do not need to be concerned with that. Only know that once you release them; you are free of them.

Chapter 6
REFLECTION

With the spiritual bank account we focus on how we have a relationship with ourselves. However, it is important to consider how we relate to others. In an ultimate mature spiritual state, one realizes that we are all connected. In our current state of development, there is still a separate mindset and a great gap in how we communicate with each other. Fear, anger, hate, pain, selfishness, and power still separate us on many levels. Until we get past those aspects of human nature, we must learn to grow in our relationships. Understanding the physical aspects of our relationships is thus necessary to our spiritual journey.

Understanding our breakdown in relationships will assist us in our communication. Relationships are great places for us to learn about ourselves. We learn from relationship failures and their successes. Those who say they have experienced a fragmented spirit connection will seem to have shut down many of their human interactions to a point that they seem to be on autopilot. Those who have experienced a broken spirit know that it is more than just disappointment, a betrayal, or the longing to create new memories. It is a sense of separation. Together we will explore the process of healing a fragmented spirit connection and the steps necessary to create life where it has been lost. Ultimately, this rebirth is the responsibility of the individual, but an understanding that creates a safe place to do that is essential. Our schools should be filled with this kind of training. We have much evolving to do in spirit.

A Fragmented Heart Connection

Most of us have experienced this in our lifetime and many have had multiple encounters with a fragmented heart connection. We connect with someone on a physical level, emotional level, and in our feelings. We may even share our thoughts with this person and create thoughts together. Rejection is hurtful. Disappointment sets in and withdrawal from usual interactions can occur. Our focus will be on what we have lost and what we wish was present. Anger sets in and if it is a relationship then some choose to hate that person or dislike them in a deep manner. Some choose depending on the event to hate or be angry with their selves. Once worked thorough people will say that they have no feeling remaining, they do not care anymore. They have resolved their expectations. This is a typical pattern of a fragmented heart connection.

A Fragmented Spirit Connection

The steps to dealing with a fragmented heart connection are similar to a fragmented spirit connection, but a fragmented spirit connection goes much further. A fragmented spirit connection is experienced when your connection to another human being or event is present in spiritual form as well as physical form on a deep level. We come to a state where we realize that we are part of the same whole. Not only do we connect on the physical plane with our emotions, feelings, thoughts, but we also connect on the spirit level where we come to a point where we have experienced a connection. This is a spiritual realization. Ultimately, our spirits are sparks of the creator and we came from the same source. On a deep spiritual level, we are one in spirit. In a relationship, you can get to a point where you experience a part of that connection. This can be understood in the physical where you are able to feel their pain with them, you are complete because of them, and you know you are complete by their presence in your life. Your spirit gets to the point where you connect with them and they become part of your identity, your desires, and the very energy you feel arise from your spirit. When two people make this connection then they have come to a realization we will never really be completely separated. It is like a glimpse of what it is like to be connected to the creator. Once this awareness is realized, it will change their experience in the physical world.

It may be possible for one person to find this connection to another human being, but the other is not yet mature enough to completely go there, they are too selfish to allow the transition, or simply were not vested. In another instance, a fragmented spirit connection can come from abuse. The fragmentation in spirit is then in relationship to itself. These causes and the symptoms can come in forms of molestation, rape, addictions, and other forms of self abuse. While we cannot attribute all behavior such as this as an exclusive indication of fragmented spirit connection, they may be present.

A fragmented spirit connection will lead to despair that is beyond simple emotion. Your spirit would rather leave this planet and dimension than to deal with its separation here. It is much like having a wound to the body. A scrape or cut is easier to heal from than a fatal wound. A fragmented heart connection is like a really painful wound that is not fatal to the human body. A fragmented spirit connection is a fractal state to the spirit. In this state the only occurrence will be an "undeath" death. In the words of one individual:

> *I would awake and this feeling would overcome me like I was anticipating seeing his face, talking as we did at that time of the day. It was like suddenly someone had told you your child was missing kind of feeling. My spirit wanted to reach out beyond my control. The fact that I would be without him was too devastating for my senses. I could not understand how he could let go. He was in my spirit, it was impossible for me not to be in his. Anything he could have done to hurt me would not compare to the separation. This death like feeling between us, but it was still alive. I needed him in my life to be complete. It is like a piece of yourself is with him and now it is not with you. He was in everything for me. Each object that we had some connection to and memory had these feelings attached to them and it was alive. It was like a hungry lion in a cage that you cannot feed. As the days go by, you expect it to get easier, but one little trigger and it grips you so intensely like you are remembering a mate that just died tragically. If they had died the grief would have been less. This was a decided separation and it was like my spirit could not breathe. I was struggling to be alive without a piece of myself.*

Part of this essential moment of realization is that a fragmented spirit connection experiences a state of forsaken life essence. One might think and ask, "why have I been forsaken?" One part of the eternal part of ourselves has been separated from us and that connection that was felt with another at that level was now a separation. One might say that they did not know at that moment how to exist after a separation from a soul connection. This connection is recognized as being part of our spirit. This is why the separation is so profound.

The relationship we create with someone else is living and breathing so to speak. We can create a stop light and it just exists as an inanimate object, but our creation in relationship is part of a living and breathing creation. We also partake in the creation process and we create with another human being. This is the most difficult aspect of a fragmented spirit connection. Being a creation of the creator, we have an essential presence in spirit that makes us complete. Without this aspect and health of the spirit, we live in separation of the source of life and thus the descent into a death that can slowly even cause a physical death as well. Stories existof a little old couple losing a spouse only to find that they die a short time later even if they were perfectly healthy a short time before. This is an example of that descent. Those two human beings were connected in spirit. In this instance, the recovery from a fragmented spirit is in an actual physical death of the human being. Then once again, they are reunited with the fragment of their spirit that was separated from them. In reality, we are never separate, but in our limited understanding we see it as so.

In many cultures, this concept is taboo or even sacrilegious, but there is a great need to address it. Death is an aspect of the physical part of our existence. The transition through death is a part of our existence in this universe. Our existence lives beyond our place in this timeline in the physical world. This experience that we are having is in interaction with our spirit. We will take our experiences and thoughts with us to the other side. Many experiencers have described it in a manner that can be summed up as a spiritual computer that downloads all our interactions and experiences while we were connected to the physical world. It is more than a simple database of information, but this information is connected to the spirit and can be retrieved in such a manner as described in death experiencers brought back to life.

Time

Time only exists for us on this planet the way that is does. If we lived on Pluto our time would be much different. Quantum science has only begun to understand that not only is there space, but there is a dimensional presence in space as well. For many years the glimpse of understanding our timeline was much like looking at a flat photograph of an object. We have now begun to understand that the actual "apple" has dimension. This mind bending concept to some is only a fantasy, but even science has begun to understand that time is relative and exists within our realm in a particular manner. The very design and existence of our world has odds of being random greater than the numbers that could fit on every page that has ever been made. Our planet is unique to us, but also our universe. Even still, we are just one universe. After my NDE, I remembered music that had no time. Time was irrelevant. Most of us have such a short lifespan on this planet. This makes time delicate and it also has great power over life. Regardless of our genes that would enable us to live for thousands of years or less than one hundred, our spirit is eternal. Even if we are given immortality in the flesh it would only be as good as the life we lead because a tragic accident would end a physical life regardless of how much youth is left.

Our spirit seeks the source when it is aware of its own state. The closest thing in this lifetime for many is to be present to the creator by connecting with another human being on that spirit level. We long for it even if we constantly send it away with our choices, attitudes, and fear. Creation in relationship to a spirit connection is created not only in our dimension, but also exists in the next dimension that is not subject to time. So when we are fragmented in connection that part of us in the next dimension is shifted as our spirit is fragmented here. This is a loss so great that those who have experienced it will say it is beyond words. That creation we made with another human being or in our own spirit is still intact in creation, but it is now separated here in the physical world. This is part of the great grief.

To further explain the concept of existing in two dimensions we can turn to monatomic elements. Monatomic gold is found to exist in two dimensions at once. They seem to break the laws of thermodynamics and have been shown to display negative mass in certain instances. Science had to ponder about where it goes. It would be much like weighing an apple and then something occurs and suddenly the apple has lost a few grams, but it looks untouched. Where did that mass go? Our spirit works like monatomic gold. It exists in at least two dimensions at once. In the next dimension, or perhaps on a much higher floor of the dimensional building, that is where the creation of this spirit connection is originated and once created there cannot die "there". Time does not exist "there" or we could say everything exists at once "there". So, when you are fragmented it is like a ripple in the connection between your spirit here and there.

Eternal Spirits

Our spirits are eternal and this point then makes this picture even more complicated. Once we leave this physical shell, we will go into another dimension which some call the "afterlife" which is another dimension. Think of a hierarchy of floors to a building. We still do not know for sure how many floors are possible in the dimensional realms, but science has seen hints of them and near death experiencers (NDE) have testimonials of a few of them. What we do know is that they exist and with rules that we have yet to understand. When I had my own NDE, I was more alive in that state than I can probably be here in this dimension. When it begins you become aware of how small your body is and your spirit feels crammed into it. This does change for you because you ***remember*** that there is something more.

Then, death is something different for you and the life after is even more of a mystery. For example, suppose you went to a play and there was a scene where someone flew across the stage. It looked very much like you have seen before. You have wondered how they did it, but the play was enough for you to be satisfied. Then one day you see the very same scene, but something changes. You suddenly see the curtain wave and realize there is a connection to the event. While you unconsciously knew this, it had yet to be tangible. You approach the back stage and you look back to see that everyone in the audience still seems to be sitting in their chairs, starring at the stage, and unaware of what you have just sensed. You walk to the curtain from behind and realize that there are all these wires and gadgets. The person controlling them was seen only in the corner of your eye and then they disappeared again behind the curtain. The next time you see a play you will have a higher awareness than those who have not seen behind the curtain. What you have also realized though is that there is far more behind that curtain than you could have imagined. There was a whole world of things that you did not quite understand or see how they interacted with one another. When you come back from this, the world is no longer black and white if it ever was to you. Things are not quite like the fairy tale on the stage or in our text books. It is a perspective that few have been aware of until they are on the other side.

Having a broken spirit connection is also like this encounter with the wires behind the stage. Once you make that soul connection to another human being you have tasted the closest thing you may find in this timeline to being in the presence of the creator. You have loved another human being on a level that was part of the creation of your own spirit's experience. Do you ever go back to just seeing the play on stage? Many of us had to do that or learned to do that, but it changes us and a part of us will never be filled with anything else in that place. There is no play that will ever completely gain our spirit's attention without the knowledge of that glimpse behind the curtain. This spirit we have exists beyond this timeline and into the next dimension. That is what makes our awareness of a spirit connection all that more painful when separated. What was created in our spirit with the other person must move on to the spiritual realm and we must stay behind. Part of our spirit then separate from us, but is never really gone.

A Broken Spirit Connection in Relationship to Others

The broken spirit that occurs because of a betrayal or separation from a spirit connection is a situation that not everyone will experience or they may experience it to different degrees. However, a spirit connection should be defined. A connection with another's spirit could take place in a romantic relationship, between parent and child, brothers and sisters, or friends. It is a connection that reaches unconditional love. For those who have not experienced this, they may actually be protected on some level. Losing this connection in the physical realm can cause a separation that can cause a human to experience pain. What is meant here is that the finding of a soul connection is not a requirement to our existence on this planet. We can love and be loved even if we are without a soul mate. There is great risk for some to take the leap to be with a soul mate. There are many who are not yet mature enough to see its value and chose someone they feel safe with or that allows them to stay where they are spiritually. They may also simply be selfishly satisfied with that level of interaction with another human being. It is even possible that it is just not needed for their experience here in this lifetime. This unawareness if we can call it that should not be seen as inferiority, but an issue of spiritual experience. We have come to this timeline to experience different things.

For those who are here and have that hunger to interact with their soul mate they then will seek to satisfy that state or may stumble on to it. What would we define a soul mate? People who have found a soul mate may say it in different words, but the essential point is that their spirits are joined in a way that exceeds the physical world. Your spirit is connected to them and separation would be a death of part of the spirit creation. They have reached out to you in the same manner and your spirits were fed. This may take a lifetime to learn for some and for others it can take little time. The first man that I thought was a "soul mate." I also thought that I would spend the rest of life with him. At the time, you could not have convinced me otherwise. Years later in life, I came to better understand the connection to another person and understood that my love and spirit connection for him exceeded his spirit awareness connection to me. I very much felt a spirit connection to him, but he did not completely reciprocate. The extent of our connection he will not truly know until he crosses over to the next dimension. He had a fragmented spirit and my love was not enough to get him thorough it. He is on his own journey.

A soul mate can be described as an individual that can be loved unconditionally. This is the true nature of our spiritual state and learning to share this state with another human being is a great experience. Some know their "soul mate", but that soul mate may have decided that they could not maintain it. They were broken. This separation will seem like more than you can bear. Yes, betrayal is there, but it will seem small compared to the separation of someone who completed you because you both shared a connection in spirit. After you have a separation from this soul mate, the world may seem as if it has lost its color. Beyond that, there is a death that begins to take place. This death must occur if we are to survive and live again. The idea that we cannot live without our "soul mate" once we know them is true in a sense. We will not be the same as we once were and must learn to be aware of the disconnect and learn to grow. There is no physical source that could satisfy, no word spoken, and no person who can fill the emptiness.

The worst part of loss after the initial grief of a loss of love is that the spirit will always long for the connection to their spirit. I do believe it is quite possible to overcome the longing for sex and physical intimacy and meet that person again only to share a spiritual connection with them. Although I will say it requires one who is mature enough to do this. When the grief process is done, we will have part of us die here in the physical world (but not the spiritual world where it lives on) and hopefully take part in a rebirth. Without that, we will slowly begin the descent into death and when our physical being can no longer carry our spirit then our spirit will find a retreat in the other side. It is a dissonance between our conscious awareness and our spiritual subconscious reality. There is no way that the part of our spirit loss will ever completely die, but it is the rebirth that holds us until we cross over. It may exist in us until then, but it is possible to reach a point where we can live a productive life and love again. My "soul mate" and I separated not that long after I had my NDE. It was that experience that reminded me that I came back for a reason and my journey was not done. Perhaps, part of me was angry as I had come back to lose what I thought was the greatest love of my life? In reality, it was my NDE as a gift that served as a reminder that there was more to come. We all make choices in life and his choice changed our paths. Now, I could change mine.

Ultimately, the reason a broken spirit is so hurtful to us is because it is likened to a part of what it means to be separated from our creator. In the spirit side, we are all connected. Those who have crossed over know this and suddenly their needs are all met. Their spirit is fed. In the physical realm, we forget this and when we connect with another human being in unconditional love, we come closer to understanding our true intended nature in the spirit. This is why it is so devastating. It is important to come to the realization that it is a lesson and place where we will appreciate the state of love all the more. It is possible that this lesson was one of the prearranged lessons that we had to experience. That is what this book is about and only the broken spirit can reach that point of realization on its own.

Spirit Manifested as Male and Female

Understanding the differences of the two sexes is helpful in communication. The spirit when stripped of the physical body is one in the same. However, while we are here in the physical we are having two distinct expressions of a spirit. These two expressions are manifested as a man and a woman. Besides the obvious physical differences, there are also manifested differences. This manifested difference is in the form of male and female. Just as cat will see the world in a certain way and a dog will see the world in a certain way depending on the manifested form they have been given. There are exceptions to these observations, however most fall into the spectrum of male or female expression. Remember that it is a spectrum and there can be exceptions.

Understanding a Woman's Brain

A woman's brain works much like a file system. When a woman is exposed to a stimulus, then her brain lights up in various places. Think of these activated parts as files. So for one emotional connection she could be creating multiple files with information in it. Her brain gets very involved with each experience with many references to each experience.

Here is an example: He suggests planning a trip to Africa to do charity work together and he suggests that they should go to South America too. "I can't wait to do that with you," he says. Suddenly the woman's brain lights up all over the place because not only has he planned a trip, but he wants to make the world a better place with her. In her mind, she now has possible multiple files and files referencing files. She may have a file for future dreams- future as in this is going to be long term. We are going to impact the world together. Then she has a folder for changing the world together with him. (hmm… can't wait to fill that folder more) . Her identity folder now has him in it. Then suddenly there is a folder for, well you get the idea. Suddenly there is a flood of hopes and aspirations. You could also see how this might lead a woman to create hundreds of folders from just a few shared experiences or aspirations. Men should be aware of this when making "promises" and plans. Women make files on those things. If you do not plan to really do those things, then don't plan for them. Women are planners and it comes naturally to them. When the man breaks it off with her then she will have to go through those files and deal with each of them individually. She will have to "unattach" to each of those concepts. A man would find this exhausting, but this is how a woman's brain works. This may shed some light on why woman often have a hard time letting go of things. So much of their being becomes involved in every experience.

Another thing that women will do when they are in mourning is question all of the information that is in each folder. From the outside it looks like she has gone mad, but actually her brain is trying to process everything that is connected to her pain now and it brings on a "virus" scan in her brain. Everything could now be suspect and surly she missed something. Her trust is broken and now she must find a reason to understand what has gone against the hundreds of folders she has created with him in it.

Understanding a Man's Brain

I remember watching a woman and man interact. To an outside observer, he was an open book. He wanted some praise from his wife. He wanted to be validated for the things he did. He wanted to be appreciated. She seemed oblivious to his core need. It was not surprising that later I heard that he had cheated on her. I would not certainly say it was an absolution for his deed, but I understand why he went looking to fill that need. Perhaps, this woman should have praised him and validated him more. She neglected feeding his spirit and was not aware.

Men desire to succeed and failure will damage their identity as a male. Being critical and judgmental will certainly cause damage. This nagging syndrome that woman can often do is damaging to any relationship. Always work to acknowledge his worth to you. Acknowledging that you believe in their ability even if he should make a mistake is what men need. They need respect. This is one of their basic needs. What men want is the support to believe in their worth and ability and that they are not disrespected or appear vulnerable in public. A woman's loyalty in public and to his circle of friends is a desire for men.

Love is manifested as respect to men, but it is also a separate aspect of love. They can say that they know they are loved, but being degraded will in effect cause a split in their confidence even if they know they are loved. Woman should ask themselves this question. Did I do this enough? Could he possible know how truly blessed I felt I was because he was in my life? Did he know that?

Trust is also an issue for men. Imagine creating one folder as they might and it says trust. There is only one folder and if there are bad things in it then he will struggle with trust possibly ongoing unless he either deletes that folder and lets it go or creates a new one. A man's brain is efficient and direct. They are very present in one particular direction in their thinking. This should be considered as a tendency.

A Fragmented Heart in Relation to Self

Having worked in a counseling capacity and as a mentor, I can say that I have seen some fragmented hearts. I have heard stories from individuals that would make an outsider think they should be broken, but somehow joy was still flowing in them. Some were robbed of their innocence by the hand of a predator. I knew one such individual whose fragmentations could not be seen by a photo or even interacting with this person in a casual manner. Deep inside, there was a place of death that may never heal for this person until they cross over, but learning to live despite it was the goal that they could hope to achieve.

A fragmented heart in relation to self can also occur. One instance is when you have made a spirit connection, but the other person has not. Your heart has fragmented against itself. What you must come to realize is that projection will be a major issue here. This can happen between two members of a relationship, between child or parent or siblings. You projected your spirit on to someone else and created and it was not reciprocated. This betrayal will leave the other person touched, but not connected. Know the difference as hard as it may seem that this statement does not validate you. While you can be completely real in your connection, there will be a point where you will see that the projection must come back inside yourself and find its home once more. The heart can also be fragmented to itself by a tragedy that has touched someone on the deepest level. This can require a defragmenting of their presence in the physical realm. Ultimately, we are responsible for our own well being. We must generate our own joy.

Joy and Happiness

Joy is an inner peace and happiness is an outward stimulus that gains our attention and gives us a temporary pleasure. We must know the difference and be sure that we always have an inner generated state of joy. We can do this by being grateful for each day and for each factor in our lives. We should be grateful for ourselves and for others. We must learn to see lessons as opportunities to learn and grow. Our attitude must be one of openness. Happiness will not fulfill our spirit. It fulfills our physical desires. The victim mentality will not allow us to be who we were meant to be. We must take personal responsibility for our thoughts, feelings, and emotions.

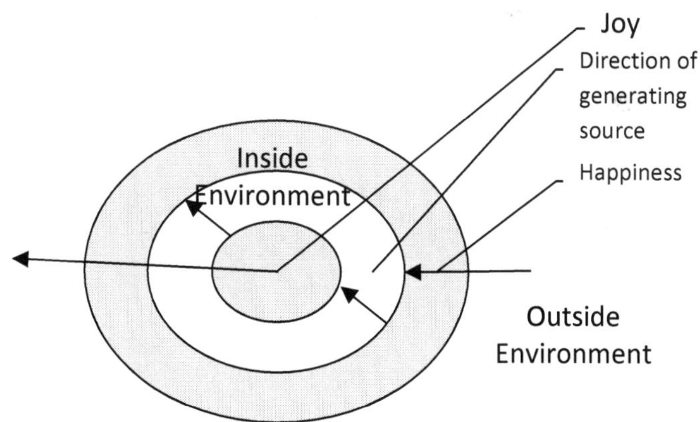

Joy/Happiness (Irene, Dianne 2012)

Chapter 7
SPIRIT CONNECTION

The first step to understanding the healing process is to understand the way that the spirit connects with the physical body and the physical realm. Everything begins with thought. From these thoughts we develop feelings. Then this feeling gives birth to emotion. Then we are ready for actions or reactions.

Spirit	This is the essence of the creator born to us as an individual being. It exists despite all the others and live on after the human body has died.
Thought	The ability of the spirit to participate in free will and its own creation process begins with thought. Thoughts exists in both the physical and spiritual realms. They are a vehicle for the manifestation of interaction with our spirit in the physical realm.
Feelings	The thoughts generate feelings and this connects us to the physical world. It is the vehicle of experiencing the thought of the spirit.
Emotions	The emotions are positive or negative expressions being expressed from the physical existence of the feelings.
Reactions and actions	The reactions and actions taken are the physical manifestation of the process above and through these stages.

Spirit Connection Hierarchy (Irene, Dianne 2004)

Spirit	This is the essence of the creator born to us as an individual being. It exists despite all the others and live on after the human body has died.
Creation matter	This is a realm of physics and quantum science. For example, human beings are still seeking to understand dark matter, string theory, and even the presence of orgone in the universe.
Physical mass	These are the very basic elements that follow their own set of laws of physical matter, but they can also be altered. They include atoms and their components.
Cells	These units of atoms work together in a creation process and are subject to known and unknown laws of the universe.
Interactive collection of physical unity	Organ systems work together for a being. They contain potential and limitations.
Physical Beings	These are made up of all of the above to manifest a functioning vehicle for a spirit to experience the physical world.

The Human being in the physical form (Irene, Dianne 2004)

The sprit is tied to both the creation as a spirit process and the physical realm process. That is where the spirit connection can overlap both aspects of an existence. Learning to understand the thought process and work through the discrepancies in each stage can lead to healing. While this is the map to healing, an individual must use their own thoughts and connection to spirit to do so. Once the process is understood, how your thoughts and feelings interact will take time with practice and patience. Soul searching is essential and sometimes asking a question will take months or years to answer or master.

Reaching Mastery

Mastery is an ongoing journey and something we should all strive for while we are on this side of existence. It is where we find a balance in our spirit and the physical creation of ourselves. Mastering the thought process and the physical process takes time and patience. Forgiving yourself is essential and not repeating our mistakes are what is not only good for us, but fair to others. Always seek to resolve your pain. Beyond the expression of many thoughts the feelings that are manifested can be broken down ultimately into two categories with all feelings being related to these two core feelings.

Feelings of Your Thoughts

Fear	Anger and pain- hate – this is a vacuum that drains life.
love	Peace and joy- This generates energy and feeds the spirit.

Fear/Love (Irene, Dianne 2004)

Evil has been a force that has been discussed throughout history. It has been set against the contrast of good. These labels have served to decipher two opposing forces. There are spiritual aspects to this concept that we now understand as positive and negative energy.

Evil in the Spiritual Realm

Evil	These are low energy sources and are draining to those who are seeking higher vibrations. They are destructive and predatory.
Hate	This is based on a deep seeded fear.

Evil/Hate (Irene, Dianne 2004)

Grieving someone can take a toll on the human spirit. It is a difficult loss and we must learn to let go of others so that we can continue on our path and fulfill our purpose. We will discuss an example and stick with the earlier example of losing a "soul mate". This general idea can be applied to other areas of loss as well.

Thought: I have lost my soul mate.

If this is your thought about the person that you have lost then the separation will spill into fear of failure, questioning contributions, and that no other replacement is possible. Deciding that this person is not your soul mate (parent, child, lover, friend) when your spirit is fed by their existence can be futile. So, instead of going down the road of finding every flaw known to man in them, it is best to reorganize.

You are my soul mate(I have loved you at the spirit level), but you have chosen a different path/you have been given a different path. Therefore I must let you go to experience a different path and realize more things about myself. I will always love you and hope that you find yourself in the end. I deserve to be loved back in a way that does not cause this pain. Therefore, I will seek new love when I have healed enough to let someone in. This does not negate my spirit connection to you, but allows me to let go of our creation together where it will once again be intact at peace on the other side. I will choose to see the beauty in life again without you because I am worthy of that.

When you accept this there doesn't need to be an immediate change. You are adding to the program that is currently running so to speak. If you chose to go down the road of hateful thoughts to undo your thinking then the journey will be much harder. Eventually you will then need to balance yourself back from that darker place. It doesn't mean that you will not get angry and feel betrayed. You see, if human beings evolved to where they should be then we would never betray each other and realize that we are all part of the same race and on the same creation level designed by the creator. The hate will only serve to fester and create a path that could lead to bitterness which will make the healing process much harder.

Bitterness is a dangerous place to go and will often follow you into future relationships. It is a place where the personality and the expression of the spirit can seem to have died. It stifles your growth as a human being and creates a victim mentality that can become an addiction in thought. You will create a mess of things to sort through in the long term.

Self Harm/ Addiction: A Growing Carnal Indication

Over many thousands of years humanity has participated in some strange and bizarre behaviors. In ancient Rome, it was common to eat an extravagant meal and then regurgitate that meal to return and eat again. In some cultures the foot is bound to keep it from growing, rings are worn around the neck to elongate it; some cultures mutilate genitals or other body parts as a justified practice. For some these practices seem cruel and are viewed as a misuse of the human body. Others feel that it is time for humanity to move beyond damaging the human body that houses our spirit. When we look at food, we should see resources to give our bodies nutrition so that we can function to the best of our ability in this vehicle that houses our spirit. The spirit is the most important aspect of caring for our bodies. Today, anorexia and bulimia are plaguing our society and destroying some of our youth.

Part of this obsession and addiction to a carnal trait as a distortion of reality needs to be carefully considered. Commercial enterprise has opened the flood gates to beauty and youth as a prized possession and made the focus of the carnal an ultimate achievement. This standard has created a subliminal message that lurks into the minds of our youth. Then, when tragedy strikes, this standard can become an outlet of choice for those that struggle to deal with real issues. This emphasizes an over exposure of an impossible standard and works like a recruiter for those seeking to gain control of an issue much deeper than the carnal. Our society's obsession with the carnal has led to the premature death of many and has halted some possible progressive leaps for the human spirit. Even more tragically, we are becoming bombarded with a profit driven medical industry more interested in increasing the bottom line than in curing or freeing someone from disease. They in turn are subject to mounds of red tape and politics. This means that those with an eating disorder may not get help or have access to a facility. This cycle only further agitates an already declining moral.

The court systems do not adequately address this addiction and often this gap leaves families struggling to find help for their family member who is committing slow suicide before their eyes. This suicide as the family sees it can last for 5 or more years or for less. Once a person becomes 18, it can become impossible to get help for an individual incapable of helping themselves. This gap must be closed if we are to save those who fall into the trap of an eating disorder. This form of addiction should be treated the same way we treat drug addicts as far as required assistance.

Also, we need woman and men to speak out about beauty and to stop allowing commercial interests to dictate what is desirable and what defines beauty. Health should always come first over beauty. This can only happen if individuals start to expand their understanding of what purpose we have on this planet. Women are not meant to be showpieces and objects of sex. Men should not be expected to be emotionless hard individuals. The lack of societal understanding of beauty is a serious problem. A woman or man's worth should always be first what is in their spirit.

Human biology will actually cause certain people to be attracted to one another. There seems to be evidence that this relates to gene compatibility. Also, some will say this is also related to preference. Just as a gorilla who speaks sign language can communicate that he or she has a preference for a certain gorilla as a partner, we too have that same tendency. However, this does not have a direct correlation to finding some stigma standard as the desired attraction. Instead, society and commercial interests have created a standard of beauty that becomes attached to an emotional state. This tragic toll on humanities' environment has been in the least a distraction to other more important standards.

These individuals who one day decide to sacrifice their health and focus on an impossible standard of perfection that is actually very far from a state of mastery; begin a journey of death. This slow form of suicide begins to distract these individuals from spiritual growth. Their world becomes consumed by food, control, and manipulation. The families of these individuals will often get locked into a cycle of enabling.

There is a real need for those leaders who are in the public eye to acknowledge a disinterest in industry standards of beauty. Expressing an acceptance and desire for health should be the focus. Again greed has played into a cycle of creation that has led to an outlet for those who get trapped in unhealthy emotional outlet. Before more individuals get recruited by the distorted cycle of coping, then we should rethink our standards of desire. Where are the ad campaigns showing how sexy a sweet man is or a woman who chooses to eat healthy and refuse junk food? Where are the role models who go against industry standards to show how the human spirit can evolve?

Dying to be thin is a symptom to a much bigger issue. It is a symptom that our society like Rome is subject to falling apart from the inside out. Just as those who focus on the carnal, they will miss life's subtle opportunities to become part of a maturing process which is a true process for our purpose in this life. It is time to get past the industry standards of beauty and desire and recognize that there is a much bigger purpose to why we have physical bodies in the first place. We are here in the physical to experience things in a way that we would not in the non-physical world. The physical world is a tool for us to learn, grow, and love. Humanity has played in the carnal for too long and it is time for us to grow up and encourage others to see true beauty in how we handle our emotional issues correctly.

Chapter 8
HUMANITIES PLACE IN CONSCIOUSNESS

Humanity has long fallen short as a race that lived in its spirit state. Most of us engage in everyday life that is full of distractions and curtains that hide reality. Let us begin with the basic human culture. In most industrialized nations, people spend most of their time pursuing the ideal life with a house, car, and career. We spend most of our time pursuing these things. In this respect, we may not realize the stunting of our spiritual growth. Many of the things that we make each other pay for is actually already ours. We just charge each other for it.

Peace for Mankind

Mankind has experienced many things throughout history. Many of us have desired for humanity to evolve spiritually and to find that humans have become loyal to other humans. Some have been given great opportunity and many blessings, but as a race we have not yet learned to stand as one race. Some souls are young in experience and others are what many see as old souls. We should be giving our children greater knowledge and training than what we have in the current generation. This should follow each generation with greater and greater knowledge. Our current education system has not been able to fully develop into this because we have allowed politics to infiltrate the sanctity of education. Each generation should be more fulfilled than the one before.

The current social issues we face on this planet are absolutely our own responsibility. As we continue on in this journey, we must understand that our place here is temporary and meaningful to our spirit's journey. No matter the outcome of the future, our spirits will go on existing. However, our choices in our world affect the future generations of lives on this planet. The suffering that we as a race face leaves a legacy for those who follow. This cycle has run a long course and now there are many who desire for the evolution of the spirit to take place. Many obstacles have been placed in our way by both our own choices and the choices of those who watch our development.

What does superiority really look like? Is being a race to suppress other races and cultures or to use the efforts of others to sustain ourselves an acceptable practice? Why is it that when there are those who begin to question the routines of society, they become a paradox to the main stream? Many have become complacent and this has caused a great slowing of our spiritual development. Now is the time to become aware of our behaviors as a race and to regroup our efforts to sustain the desires of the soul. Remember that while we have classes and races that are seen as superior to others that this has only served to keep us from evolving as one race and as spiritual beings. In spirit, there is no class, no race, no carnal wealth, and no keepers of power over others.

We live in a world where currency has deemed the powerful and the clever as rulers of events. However, as beings in this timeline, the real currency we have is time. It is time that runs and time that ages. It is time that runs out in this lifetime to see our children play and speak in sweet voices. It is also time that heals and grants our understanding to experience. We should savor time as a gift that when ignored becomes a burden.

In the ideal world we are creatures of personal responsibility with the desires of personal determination. We see the world through our eyes and our spirit. We do not look to angels to save us from the dark, but stand in faith and confidence that we are given a sacred spirit that can express the beauty that our creator has given us. We have a great desire to use unconditional love to teach, guide, and create. We remember what we are in this universe. Humans are a creation who embraces love and releases pain and fear.

The time has come for humanity to stop and listen to the spirit. Each one of us has that inner voice that speaks and those voices that come from a higher place. We need to listen and listen soon. Do not hesitate to feel and sense the truth. Move away from what others say and sit and listen. Think and feel. It is essential that humans do not consume too much distraction with the daily entertainments and rituals of daily life. Realize that what others do around you is a place for them and that your place is one that is created for you. Inner peace can only come from taking inventory and understanding that a connection is necessary at the soul level with all that has been given to us by the creator. This beautiful planet that was given to us and all its inhabitance are our companions. We have what we need to live. There is water, food, and an environment that was given to us. We should not have to pay to live with what has already been given to us by the creator. However, some have become greedy and created a system that locks us into a systematic existence.

Our currency system has kept us from realizing that what is here is already ours. It is our mindset that is flawed. We bought into this system. Instead, we could live in a place where we do what we do because we love to do it. We challenge ourselves to improve our systems and creations. We do it for the next generation that we create responsibly and with great reverence as parents of sacred souls. When we deprive others then we deprive ourselves. We belong to each other. We should remember that we are creating our future by the choices that we make today. Peace is in living in our spirit and knowing that it is where we will return.

Opportunity in a Time of Trouble

There is great opportunity in front of us at the present. The world is changing from what we know to be the current reality. We are now more aware of how we treat our planet, animal life, and even our fellow human beings. Some of us feel that pull to become more aware and more sensitive to what is going on around the planet. Some look around and see the monetary system failing and think that it is the basis of society. How can we function without a monetary system? If we look into the deep recesses of ourselves, we will see that this system is a superficial one that we have grown accustomed to as members of society. However, we know that it is a temporary value and that human beings far outnumber the value in a monetary system. Anyone who could deny this is denying themselves. While this may seem like a futuristic fantasy, it is where the race on this planet should be going. It means that we should be developing communities where we care for each other and work together. Imagine if humans were no longer a controlled being who had to participate in the daily grind of work, school, and pressures of complying with the process of daily life.

Let's look even deeper; shall we? Beneath the flesh, we are spirit. This is the part that makes us animated. It is the immortal part of us. Even if we are removed or disconnected from our current bodies we would then experience reality without them. The point here is that we are not our bodies and they are not us. We are much more in the sense of creation. We are immortal spirits living in a flesh reality until we wear out or are separated from that body. Some people have realized this truth after a near death experience where they were able to bring back memories of a glimpse of what is beyond the veil of the physical realm. Some of us are sensed to be old souls and young souls and this is not that far from the truth. As immortal beings, we will not be destroyed and will live on from the time we are created.

Now, the physical realm has been the only conscious reality for many in this lifetime and any memories of eternity are not conceivable to them. They struggle with everyday life and their values are in the carnal things. They are not evil, just not aware of what is beyond the veil. Knowing this immortal secret would bring their reality to a new place where they would appear to grow as a spirit by leaps and bounds. However, in reality they are really just asleep and unaware and this growth would be an awakening. As spirits, we know this truth and need only to awaken to its reality. At that point they can choose denial or embrace it. If they chose the path of denial, they will struggle and deep inside feel fragmented. This can trace their behaviors to a variety of carnal traits. If they choose to embrace this reality then they will soon become aware that they no longer fit into the daily reality.

At this point, the search for the truth usually begins. Some find their peace of mind in saturation of the current reality. Others begin to explore what some term as "outside of the box". This brings about the reality that there may be more than one reality. Those who are capable of seeing multiple perspectives usually catch on to this reality more easily. The sense of a personal awareness and self responsibility is a part of this awareness. We are eternal beings that exist despite the rules and realities we now face. Therefore they should not define us or confine us to control from outside forces. We are responsible for our spirit and its journey. Allowing others to take control of our destinies and desires will only hinder our development as a unique spirit on a journey of growth and exploration. After all, this physical journey should not be wasted by being locked into someone else's perspective.

Some spirits have come to this reality and seem to have been given great opportunity and earthly wealth. From the modern societal perspective, this puts the masses at a disadvantage. We view it this way because we are living in their reality. Their values have become our values. Money, fame, and power are at the forefront of many of the stories of history. This is because their reality has been repeated over and over again. However, we are no more disadvantaged than they are at any point in spirit. We would not be at any disadvantage in the physical realm either if we were more aware and more responsible for our own well being.

How can this realization be applied in a practical way? We need to take care of each other. If you awake to discover that the monetary system has completely failed ask yourself if you would be willing to do what you do to take care of each other? Imagine if you lived in a community were money was not all that necessary, but resources were utilized to create harmony. Then who would be wealthy? Who would be powerful? Life was not meant to be part of a slave system of debt and control.

The environment is our home and we are its inhabitance. Just as those who oppress truth for power so too those who have been harsh to our environment are trading harmony for disharmony. Everything that is done is and will exist. There are two sides to this reality. One is that it exists as part of our history once something occurs, but the other is that it also is a fleeting reality in the physical realm. The consequences in the physical realm will take precedence in the physical sense. However, the spirit in the dimensional realm will follow the laws of dimension. Even those that some have seen as gods will merely be subject to the same realities in the spirit as those they have suppressed. Pain inflicted upon the weak will translate into feeling that pain caused from their perspective in the face of truth. No one escapes the behaviors or truths of reality in spirit. Even in the physical realm they may claim victory and arrogance, but truth is immutable in spirit. While some have evolved in knowledge and understanding, they have not taken their role as teacher seriously. They have held on to their morsels of golden knowledge as if it belongs to them. Truth belongs to no one and exists in itself. Therefore it is for everyone at all times.

So, if society awakes one day and there is no source of money then look to these thoughts and remember that we all contain the capacity to care for one another in choice and in spirit. The choice is ours to make. Communities of individuals are a far better choice than chaos and madness. Far too long we have relied on an artificial system and now is the time to consider things that are "outside the box". Do not be afraid to reach out to your neighbor and care for each other. Do not keep score and certainly do not think like the machine of "monetary enslavery" that has led us here in the first place. Millions are losing their homes, their jobs, and their careers. As human beings let us not lose our humanity and what we are capable of as stewards of the truth. Energy should be free, our resources should be used wisely, and humans should be cared for and nurtured. Anything less is well, un-evolved.

Citizens of the Ecosystem

The concept of going green has been gaining attention in the media and in marketing campaigns from a growing number of companies. This concept continues to become the conversation that businesses are discussing. Going green means that society will have to consider renewable resources, cleaning up poor environmental practices, and taking a serious look at responsibility.

As a human race, many things have been done to impact our environment. We have made technological advances that have given way to conveniences and advances. However, humans have taken some routes of advancement that have not been environmentally responsible. Our ecosystem relies on a balance of factors. Upsetting this balance eventually affects the whole ecosystem. *The Energy Solution Revolution* was written Dr. Brian O'Leary a former US astronaut with NASA and a scientist that taught at Princeton, Berkeley, and Cornell. He reminded us that free energy is not out of reach, but already exists and must be openly accepted soon. Humanity must embrace energy sources that do not harm life and the planet. He states that this is a "wake up call" to change the culture of the planet from domination by "capitalistic self-interest, pointless wars, ecocide and dirty energy", where the majority of humanity can join together with compassion for all life. He states that we must do this before it is too late. Dr. O'Leary visited various scientists that have successfully demonstrated machines that produce zero point energy. These machines produce more energy than what is required to run them. They are clean and can run without the need for fuel and would lead to personal independence.

Free energy became a passion for Dr. O'Leary as well as protecting the planet. We spoke about free energy. He had a great understanding of how it operated and we discussed some of the concepts. We even discussed using a scientific perspective of crystalline energy. Perhaps, in the future instead of thumb drives, we will have crystals that store our data. This is just one application idea. Most importantly, no matter how scientific his discussion was, it came back to the idea that we must use technology in harmony with the planet, others and for peace. Late in his life he retired to South America and became an advocate for Ecuador's rainforests and addressed the United Nations. He worked to be an advocate for the planet. He traveled and spoke around the world about how we could improve our environment and lives by being in balance with each other and our environment. He was a strong natured Irish man that had a gentle side that those who knew him could see. Until his last year of life, he worked with integrity in promoting a better way for humanity. While those that are often in the media that pass on get a great deal of attention after their death, Brian slipped away quietly, but those that knew him knew that we lost a hero to the planet and scientist with a heart.

ENERGY Discussion

Energy consumption plays a role in varying factors related to our environment, life, and economy. Current sources should be reconsidered. Just a few sources are considered below as there are others that should be considered including magnetic energy:

- Solar
- Fission
- Fusion
- Wind
- Clean Burning Alcohol

Energy

We currently have many nuclear plants in the US and around the world. Simple common sense tells us that these are very dangerous to our environment and to human and animal life. Chernobyl should have served as a serious wake-up call to the energy community. However, not much has changed and they should be held accountable. In the days of grade school when energy was introduced in science class, we were told about the sun's energy, fusion, fission, and if we were lucky alternative energy sources. If we stop and think for a moment, why would we rape our planet? Even the most skeptical of us would acknowledge that the food chain is affected by environmental factors. Who would not want an energy source that is free, non-polluting, and runs the least risk for environmental concerns? The answer to this is simple. Our technological advancement alone warrants our move beyond this ignorance.

Solar

In my travels, I met an interesting man who I hesitated to let in. He was very grandfatherly in his appearance and spoke like a man with a genius IQ. He was very skilled at saying things without saying them. This was most likely some of his training as a government analyst that we will call "Bob". He had extensive experience with energy sources and he clearly stated that it is time to change our energy sources or face serious consequences. This individual explained that after years of experience with nuclear plants, oil fields, and other energy related sources as well as events, his conclusion was that we should convert the all plants to solar immediately. He confided in me that radiation has leaked into the environment and the water shed. He said that cancer would continue to rise. He said that it may already be too late. He was also in strict opposition to the use of oil. He made it clear that there are several schools of thought on what we should do and that even "they" were not in agreement. We discussed how solar could be used. In reality, we could take one of the western states and set up a solar hub that would collect all the energy needed for the United States. This energy can be stored and dispersed. This could be a free energy source. Imagine little old ladies not worrying about their energy bills! Now this should excite those that truly are in the energy business to create energy. We also discussed water and how it is very important for humans to use water that has been cleansed by reverse osmosis. Creating clean sources of energy would contribute to cleaner water for everyone. He indicated that our water shed was in serious trouble.

Fission

When I taught mathematics for several industries, I would have discussions with some of the engineers. I became good friends with one such engineer. We discussed nuclear power. I remember having discussion about why it was "wrong". His argument was that this advancement was worth the risk. I asked him if Chernobyl was worth the risk. I asked him if it had the potential to harm human life if it was worth the risk. I tried to be sensitive knowing that he had worked on nuclear devices and had great respect for the intricacies of nuclear energy. However, he did yield when we discussed the fact that human life if far more sacred than scientific advancement. We had great respect for each other, and I often looked at him as a father figure, so our disagreement on this issue did not hinder our discussions on technological advancement. My stand had been that if we can not contain the radiation then we have no business creating the power. This is something that Einstein realized before he died and regretted the harm that might come about from the knowledge he was encouraged to explore. In his final days, he focused on quasi-science and has been quoted as trying to understand the mind of God.

Fusion (Current Cost- Billions)

Fusion fuels have often not gotten as much attention as fission. The only acceptable form of fusion would be one that releases no neutrons and thus would not be a danger of radiation contamination. Dr. Bussard, a pioneer in fusion, indicates that the only proper fuel in fusion energy would include 3 helium atoms and no neutrons released and where the source would be heavy isotopes of hydrogen. He also indicates that the Helium 3 could be recycled back through an exhaust system. The molecules must be thrust together within a very small space to get the fusion to take and a strong magnetic force has been achieved using a magnetic confinement machine. The "bumping" of particles need about 1000 "jumps" to create a fusion.

The current approach of fusion is highly radioactive, expensive, the machines are giant, and unpredictable results are obtained. However, in nature, fusion exists in the stars and the sun. By looking at this process in nature, we can see that it uses gravity as the force to bring the particles together in fusion. Nature does this in an efficient way. Dr. Bussard wishes to use this as an example to create fusion with an electric field force that would act like gravity. This "Electric Fusion" would contain a core where the fusion would take place. This space would be significantly smaller than current methods. It would utilize quasi-spherical magnetic fields which trap the electrons and then the ions would be oscillated across the "core" until fusion takes place. Dr. Bussard indicates that this system would be like a "spherical colliding-beam device". The fusion material would then form in the system walls while the fuel gas input would be at well edges. He also discusses another approach, using the ion fusion power generating in the central region including the "wiffel ball" effect, "magrid" effect with consideration of effectiveness. After much engineering for a device, they created one that they feel would take this method to more practical applications.

He feels that this energy method should yield cheap or free electric power, be clean "burning", that ethanol would replace gasoline; it would create a possible burn for nuclear waste, use fresh water from the sea, and have many other benefits. Dr. Bussard feels that the third world nations would then become an economic player by creating the cane crops used in this process. He also sees that this would destroy the gasoline market and eliminate the oil cartels. Desalination plants would become cheap and clean water would then encourage agriculture. He even credits this invention with ending the wars of the Middle East which he calls, "Oil Wars". He indicates that the profit potential could also be as high as 100 billion per year.

The only clean fusion method includes:
P + 11B--- 3 4He Output= 8.70 mgV
6Li +6Li --- 3 4He (p, 2He cycle) Output =10.44MgV

*It should be noted that according to Bussard all other combinations give off some form of harmful radiation and should therefore not be considered.

These methods however, are still in development and not yet ready for commercial use. Also, the production cost is extensive and concerns of raw materials that might be dangerous must be considered. While this discovery is good news to current nuclear production, other forms of future energy production that are more benign should be considered. Even a plant such as this could still have dangers to humans and the environment if energy is not controlled. This also does not free humans from larger corporate power companies.

Wind

Wind is free, renewable and stable. This source of energy is really better for our environment than even clean burning fusion. There is no risk of explosion and repairs can be made very easily. The maintenance costs are even low once established. T. Boone Pickens advocates such a resource and has recently stood against the odds to bring the discussion of wind power to the table. He indicates that our use of oil is growing at a staggering rate. In 1970, the US imported 24% and the import is now in the neighborhood of 70%. A 2005 study conducted by Stanford University concluded that the abundant potential for wind power would satisfy global needs at least 7 times the current need. Pickens believes the investment to build wind turbines in the high wind areas of the US would pay off and be worth the initial investment. His campaign is growing and gaining national attention. While there are many who have advocated this for many years, it just might take a powerhouse individual like Pickens to get results. http://pickensplan.com)

Clean Burning Alcohol

David Blume, an ecological expert, has addressed the issue of the prohibition and what he calls its true purpose. The model A and T car was a duel fuel system and could burn both alcohol and oil/gasoline. With the push for prohibition, the oil industry got an 18 year head start that allowed its establishment to what we know today in the industry. The use of alcohol is clean burning and can be made from numerous sources including apples. This source of fuel could be made locally, is relatively inexpensive in comparison to oil, and would make people independent of large corporate controlled fuel sources. The idea is that as long as we have the sun then plants would participate in photosynthesis and then be able to be turned into a usable alcohol fuel. A distillery was standard equipment on farms in the onset of the agricultural movement. Farmers could them make their own alcohol, to light the home, as a solvent, and as a fuel. The advent of gasoline from oil first started in the cities and the duel fuel was necessary for those traveling back and forth. With the push of the prohibition, a switch to gasoline then became the only fuel source for vehicles. The first cars using alcohol had 105 octanes and gasoline only had 50. Even from the beginning, alcohol fuel was obviously superior, good for the environment, and less expensive and less likely to be subject to a monopolized control. Henry Ford once said, "if we can't be the farmers customer, how can he be ours?" He was opposed to the gasoline movement and is said to have had disputes with its founder. Unfortunately, with a 4 million dollar donation from a private donor, the Women's Christian Temperance Movement fought to pass prohibition. This stopped the manufacturing of alcohol for any reason.

This same movement was attempted in France and Germany with no success. Perhaps, this has even influenced our attitude towards alcohol today. In Germany around the 1800's, they were using alcohol as fuel. They started cooperative alcohol fuel distilleries. This aided in keeping the potato market stable. In return, you would get 1/3 of the alcohol back. A mash byproduct could also then be used as a fertilizer or feed. Germany could then export this alcohol, get rid of their subsidies, and it was good for the environment. They even produced alcohol burning vehicles. Paul Federate, a representative of American farmers, went to Germany to help learn how to build these distilleries. He came back to America and the farmers gathered at the Washington Grange, but unfortunately, the state police were called in by a private citizen. They arrested the grangers as they sang the Star Spangled Banner. They were accused of having dangerous German ideas. The plans were confiscated. It was many years before the idea was revisited. Standard Oil was broken up in 1911 accused of being a monopoly and tried in federal court. The four successor companies were Exxon, Mobil, Amoco, and Chevron. Alcohol can also be made out of waste "food". The sugar is a food for the yeast that makes the alcohol. This method can produce 192 proof alcohol for about 30 cents per gallon. 1/3 of alcohol is oxygen, requires less oxygen to burn, and may need an engine adjustment to take advantage of an earlier firing of the fuel.

The current energy uses are heavily reliant on a costly market of dangerous and often non- renewable resources. Exploration of alternative energy sources is both viable and essential to the environment, wildlife, and humanity. The lack of development of solar, wind, and non-radiating fusion have contributed to the lack of "varietied" sources for consumers. Our environmental decline has become a serious indicator of our lack of tolerable energy sources. It has become necessary to address this issue with more than discussion and to move to an action plan that will move the culture of energy to a new era.

The Great Garbage Patch

The Great Garbage Patch, a mass conglomeration of floating garbage estimated to be more than the size of Texas, is threatening our ocean and its wildlife in a serious way. The real culprit to this hazard is plastic. Our environment suffers when plastic is not properly disposed or recycled.

Now, scientists are examining the Pacific Ocean with great concern and finding wildlife with plastic in their systems. These creatures are suffering from plastic poisoning and the fish are not safe to eat. This great travesty is truly irresponsible and needs to be cleaned up. The other issue to consider is that this should not have happened in the first place. This is just one factor in how humans have been predatory towards the planet. Be encouraged to research the extreme dangers of the nuclear industry, how oil drilling affects the planet, and how we are consuming faster than the planet can sustain. Educating yourself on these issues is vital to understanding real issues of surviving and thriving on this planet and with each other.

It is important to address this issue as citizens of this planet and ensure that this and other environmental disasters do not happen again. Going green does not just mean that citizens just accept the idea, but that the concern moves into action and responsibility. It should not be seen as a fad, an excuse to gain attention, but as a way to take responsibility as citizens of the ecosystem.

Empowerment Strategies

Empowerment is the most evolved form of power. Empowerment establishes a perspective to view what is important and why. Awareness of the power in empowerment is in how you react to those choices and in recognizing a responsibility in choosing them. A transformation in growth can be achieved by making a conscious assessment of the perspectives that are reflective of the strengths and weaknesses of more than one perspective.

Beyond self-protection are recognition and the ability to give recognition to others. Feeling secure enough to allow a focus on the other party and their situation with a greater understanding is a key step in reaching empowerment. Channeling what may be seen as aggressive attacks from another party as a response of frustration and self-preservation allows room for better communication. Moving from a negative approach to a more enlightened awareness of what the other party may actually be contributes to peace. Establishing a balance of our identity is the key to where we embrace and adapt to the needs of others and ourselves. Sometimes not reacting can be a powerful response allowing another force to have the room to seek balance. Compassion can even lead to a positive resolution. Resolutions will not always be reached, but the process can be beneficial with understanding being achieved. Empowerment lends itself to the place where we can obtain the ability to better handle conflicts and reach personal growth.

Motivation

Motivation is a strong force behind actions. Recognizing intrinsically or extrinsically rooted motivation enables one to obtain a more consistent performance. Behind every action is a purpose and behind every purpose is a motive for action. Motivational Psychology is one of the most sought out philosophies of managerial training. Without the understanding of motivation, empowerment is stifled, communication is weakened, and efforts can be wasted.

Realizing the motivational drive behind a work force has led successful businesses to longevity of excellence. Those companies who have neglected worker motivation eventually become catalysts to a mundane working machine where the mechanics of a work force resemble a factory rather than a growing working entity with common motives. Understanding why one does rather than if one did is a much bigger return on worker productivity.

Personal Development & Motivation

There have been those in history who have achieved a form of mastery. We celebrate those individuals as legends, geniuses, spiritual beings, and philosophers. However, many of them have been prosecuted, killed, and considered crazy, yet their contribution has been essential to truth, spirit, and thought. When we have embraced this, then understanding our purpose is realized.

Our schools should be filled with opportunity to think about history critically and not memorize a perspective given by someone on a different journey. We can stop poverty, we can cure cancer, we can save the environment, we can end war, we can feel other's pain, and we can be kind. Each master has realized that they can take responsibility for their own choices, attitudes, and perspectives. We should be careful not to judge other's beliefs. It serves a purpose in their life. Their journey is created for them and we should be concerned with our own journey, our own responsibilities, and our own desires.

There is a shift happening. Can you feel it? This shift is at a crossroads of existence. Now is the time for us to choose a very direction for our universe. We need to break out of our superstitions, our fears, and our selfishness. It begins with thought. That is why educating yourself is so important. All the things we create here in our physical realm have started with a thought. When enough people start to wake up then action will follow.

We have the power to create a better world. We have the power to create a better self. Now is the time. Our environment in dire need, our people are starving. Yes, our people, because we belong to each other. Nothing we do in life is solely for us. It all has a ripple effect that affects the universe. Think about how a smile can change a person's day. Think about how paying attention outside what everyone else is doing and saying could mean for humanity.

Real Success in Leadership

What makes someone great and memorable? Is it becoming a title to an article in the future, being a household name, being the first to invent something, or even being able to keep a prestigious job for a period of time? Perhaps, what makes us great is our ability to "do" with character. This leads to the point of what makes a real team player who can focus on the big picture and see a vision for the future.

What separates those who have achieved in a system from those who have arrived to the human element is a sense of growth that lends itself to that unspoken character element. Some define truly arriving in their careers as achieving a large office, supervising others, or even getting a raise. However, when the day is done it is the knowledge of who we really were in those moments of success and in obstacles that will reveal our character and essentially who we really are as professionals.

What kind of leader are you? It is easy to be good to others when there is prosperity, but it is those who show poise when things get difficult that are displaying true leadership practices. The human element should never be forgotten under any circumstance. At the end of the day, we are all part of a family, have hopes and dreams, and stories of our own. The most important aspect of a person's career is the legacy of integrity and empowerment that is left behind.

- Always communicate the truth. Anything less will eventually corner you.
- Practice positive speech even in a heated discussion. This leads to resolution. Negative speech only leaves rifts that are unproductive.
- Make sure that you continually seek out different perspectives. Someone who only sees one side is not practicing leadership.
- Remember that winning is not a goal, but rather resolution and growth. Then prosperity will come.

• Say you are sorry when you make a mistake. Then make it right.
• Don't judge others by your personal expectations.
• Don't blame an individual for your lack of group success. Take responsibility and regroup.
• Focus on solutions and not on problems.
• Realize that micromanagement is for small children and not for adults.
• Offering something to others in the form of service or advice even if you are not selling them something creates value.
• Sometimes those who speak the least have the most to gain.

Humanities Addiction to Greed

Over many hundreds of thousands of years, humanity has repeated many behaviors. Advancements are made only to have them regulated, controlled, and oftentimes only made available to a few. If humanity was been given this time to develop how can we still be in the place where cancer is not eradicated, poverty is rampant, people work their entire lives to pay off something called debt? The answer boils down to a very simple human desire. One would hope that after all these years; humanity would have gotten beyond greed.

Greed is a simple human desire; however its roots infiltrate many aspects of humanity. When we look back in history we can see many examples of greed. Glorious Rome had accomplished what many cities could have only dreamed of accomplishing in the way of the arts, architecture, economy, and even technology. Humans had developed these advances only to allow them to be misused and for gratitude to become the missing link.

One of the greatest civilizations was torn apart ultimately by greed. The addiction to greed led to an obsession with power and ultimately, the demise of the great city. The lesson that humanity can learn from the past of Rome is pertinent to our future.

Our economy is no longer based on a value of gold; it instead has become a fast working machine of greed and control. Humanities entire concept of money has led us to a form of modern slavery and to modern monarchy. The wealth has been accumulated by the few and the many work to keep a monetary machine in working order. Benefits are given to those high in the game and those that are common, are left with a treadmill path of debt and earnings.

Our planet was given to humanity to enjoy, care for, and be stewards of the other creatures that also occupy the planet. This should never be part of a political ideology to gain monetary power. The sacredness of what we have been given has gotten lost in the elements of our monetary mentality. Nature is a gift for all of humanity.

The "Sides" of Greed

Humanity has enough land to accommodate everyone. The planet could easily provide a renewable crop bed for the entire world in the growth of vegetation. Instead, we are progressing to the mass manufacturing of living creatures in a large factory process which actually puts strain on the environment and leaves less room for renewable crop growth. Humanity has also commercialized the concepts of health. A great monetary component to our working machine, the health care system has become a club where only those who have access can benefit from its offerings. Alternative medicine has been considered like the "atheistic club" of a religiously rigid mindset. This tragic attitude has stunted the opportunities that both schools of thought have in curing the world of its ailments. Much like political systems of two sides, they are in an endless battle to be the source of contribution. Instead, we should be moving beyond "sides" to a place where the thought process is sacred and the decisions are to the benefit of humanity.

The political system has been commercialized and fallen into the trap of sides. If each one served and left their office with no benefits, then how quickly would their decisions for humanity be prioritized? Those that serve should still be subject to the collective priority. How can a political system that is exempt from the laws they pass be the best source for decision making? The idea of sides, has served to separate the power of the people to be citizens of planet earth. The politics in politics is not necessary and could be sufficiently fixed if the terms were really a service and not an entitlement.

Entitlement

When those who are in groups exempt themselves from the collective, then they create a form of slavery mentality. The commercial machine begins then to serve itself and get caught up in the survival of itself. The very purpose for its function is lost to greed. The monetary system should, however, never be used to enslave man's free will of enterprise. However, greed has allowed the "politicalization" of many schools of thought. Entitlement is an attitude that feeds the greed process. All of humanity is on a journey and each of us is entitled to be personally responsible for our journey. No system should dictate our spirit's path. However, when entitlement causes the suppression of others, then it has become an element of the human body that refuses to acknowledge its true function in that body.

Together, we have the talents, the resources, and the ability to create a fair and prosperous life for everyone, yet we still have to even eradicate hunger. This real problem could be satiated. Instead, we still have parts of humanity that are dying from hunger. This is brought about by the mentality of entitlement. We should be following the resources back to the source and realizing that our resources belong to humanity. They should never be patented, owned, and held for profit. Water, land, and vegetation should be considered sacred rights and should never be commercialized and accessed by only the few. This very dangerous mentality will only stunt the physical well being of the planet and it people, but also present the realization that humanity still has not matured.

The Same Source

Humanity can keep repeating the Rome path and being caught in the fear of self preservation, or we can start acting like one race on this planet that remembers that we all came from the same source and it is to this one source that we will return. The humbling realization that what we create is our own responsibility and that we are all accountable in spirit in how we interact with others and what we do for humanity is not an option, but a reality. The sooner we embrace this truth, the sooner life on this planet will become what it was meant to be and the people will become aware of who they really are and that we are indeed free to not choose greed.

Population Debate

Some groups feel that there are too many of us. Some feel that it is the incorrect use of resources that is the problem. Some feel that if it is an issue then why are we not addressing it openly? Some feel it is utter nonsense. No matter what your stance is on this issue, it is important to think about the consequences of all sides of thinking.

The first thing we must acknowledge is that all human life has value. Reducing the population by strategic reduction will not even be an acceptable solution for those leaders who are spiritually mature. That kind of thinking is the kind of focus that shadows Hitler and others like him. Hitler was not an evolved human being. While he was brilliant, his spiritual development was seriously lacking. Instead, looking at how resources are used and how to responsibly procreate should be the focus.

One of the factors to consider is that we are not self-sufficient. It is very realistic to consider the consequences this has had on the planet and society. If each community or family grew more of their own food, produced their own electricity in environmentally friendly ways, and took personal responsibility for their own welfare, then this world would be a much better place. This is the ideal that we should strive for and soon. The mass production of energy and agriculture in harmful ways has taken a toll on our ecosystem. It has caused a great deal of greed and hardship to humanity. The fact that our race has not taken responsibility on this issue is unacceptable and now is the time for action.

Many people have migrated to cities creating areas of high population. In these circumstances, you will find an effect on the human body. One example of this is that males will increase their testosterone production and thus, be more susceptible to stress and violence. Most people appreciate the convenience of city life and this is understandable, but we have not designed them with the concern for human development in mind. Cities should be designed in harmony with the environment and consideration should be taken for the affect it has on its inhabitance. The ancient architects actually designed buildings in conjunction with the sun to utilize the best source of light. Many of these buildings are still standing and have served as an example of their great skill. Yet, humans have allowed greed and monetary gain to create cities of crowding and pollution. Buildings are not built to last thousands of years and to function as a sanctuary for humanity. If we built correctly, then we would not have to build so often and at the expense of the ecosystem.

Another concern is about those who feel that strategic reduction is an acceptable behavior behind closed doors. Once such reference to this is made by Jacques Cousteau from the UNESCO Courier (1991), and it states, that one American was more burdening than twenty citizens from Bangladesh. He stated that it was awful to say this, but more awful not to say it. He believed that population needed to be balanced by eliminating 350,000 humans daily.

A report given at an international conference revealed that damaged sperm is now produced by about 85 per cent of men (Murray, 2001). According to Aitken (1999), there is now evidence that there is an increase in reproductive issues with men in the last several decades. He reports that there is a rise in testicular cancer and poor sperm quality. This factor whether it was purposely planned or not, means that the balance that keeps the natural process of procreation in balance could be in danger.

Another interesting observation can be made in the Georgia Guidestones. Located on a hill in Elbert County these granite stones were reportedly taken from a pyramid and contain commands for an "age of reason". They are written in many languages. The guided messages are as found on Wikipedia:

- Maintain humanity under 500,000,000 in perpetual balance with nature
- Guide production wisely improving fitness and diversity
- Unite humanity with a living new language
- Rule passion-faith-tradition and all things with tempered reason
- Protect people and nations with fair laws and just courts
- Let all nations rule internally resolving external disputes in a world court
- Avoid petty laws and useless officials
- Balance personal rights with social duties
- Prize truth-beauty-love-seeking harmony with the infinite
- Be not a cancer on the earth-leave room for nature- leave room for nature

These guides sound like some good ideals, but imagine if one group got to decide who that 500 million got to be and how do we get down to that number?

The population issue is a controversial one, but one that cannot be ignored. Humans cannot allow a group of people to selectively choose who should live or die like Hitler did, nor can we continue the practice of misusing the earth's resources. Our solution lies in responsible procreation and creating children that families intend to love and raise properly, and in taking personal responsibility for ourselves and our family, becoming independent and using the earth's resources responsibly, and never forgetting that human life is valuable and deserves to be treated with dignity and sanctity.

Letting Go of Darkness

There are those who thrive on darkness. They enjoy the excitement and the power. Chaos is their symphony and life is a game. However, there is a growth shift in the human population at present. This shift is a realization that as a collective, we can take personal responsibility and begin to embrace the positive aspects of life. Humanity is at an exciting time in history. Those who are focusing on the negative will be consumed by the negativity and those who are refocusing their efforts on possibilities will begin to understand more of whom they are and that we are all connected.

This means that humanity is beginning to see past the stereotypes, the facade of politics, the greed, and the uncaring attitude towards others. The color of skin, cultural differences, religions, and status are losing their separation power. People are awakening to their conscious minds. The auto pilot of unconsciousness is lifting and humanity is seeking a better life for our world. The boxes of labels, schools of thought, and superstitions are becoming transparent.

There will be those who choose not to be part of this growth process and it is their choice. However, there are those who are searching for this awakening and desire for maturing. This means that we are on the tipping point of a leap in history. This is a time where we can move into a more mature, kind world, or we can go back to sleep and allow this opportunity to pass and allow those who are negative to define humanity.

The great philosophers of the past like Martin Luther King, Mother Teresa, Kubler Ross, Nicola Tesla, Jesus, Aristotle, Buddha, Leonardo da Vinci, Gandhi, and others would be truly delighted at the progress in spirit of some of humanity. There is a desire to stop practicing destructive behaviors and move into a place where we recognize the blessings of this world and treat them as a sacred place in all of our lives. Despite the push of hate between some groups, there emerge those who are expressing love and kindness.

No doubt, the Jews, and the Hungarians, Austrian, Polish, and German "traitors" to Hitler who experienced Auschwitz may have seen the world ending for them and thought that the world was doomed, but Hitler was removed from power. The Christians that were fed to lions in Rome must have believed that humanity had stooped to its darkest level. The citizens of Japan who were stuck in the middle of a war may have believed that when Hiroshima was bombed that it was the end of the world. Africans and those who have been sold into slavery and treated as if they were objects must have felt that humanity was barbaric, immature, and cruel. However, life did go on and those that survived outside of these events continued to contribute to humanity. They should serve as lessons that we should never repeat.

In modern times, we have received warnings that it was the time to change our ways. The gulf oil spill, the nuclear disasters of Japan, Chernobyl and Three Mile Island, Nebraska among others, the Great Garbage Patch, the mass bird and fish deaths, the disappearing fish, the famines, the genocides, the biological manipulation of food, the religious wars, and the failing political and monetary systems have all served to awaken many. Some have paid attention and have begun an awakening, while others have chosen to stay asleep. Some who have been on the operating side of these events are there waiting for their next step. We must usher in a way for them to come and be part of our solution and part of humanity. They are our brothers and sisters of humanity and love is their answer.

For those who choose darkness, there is a need that they have that is at the spirit level. Fear, power, self preservation, entitlement, greed, and hate can all be cured by love. Those who have wronged humanity and promoted harm should know that love is for them as well. They too should be allowed to come into the fold and seek asylum and restitute their actions to help heal humanity and the planet. Those of oil, nuclear, chemical, poisons, the greedy, groups who have caused violence and hatred, and oligarchy groups are all part of humanity. Much like an injured part of the body, they need to be attended and healed. As long as we judge and send them hate, they will not heal. Instead, if like a seed, these words make their way into the hearts of those who know them and they begin to build a bridge then humanity can heal and begin to work together for our future. The time for sides and opposing teams has grown short and the separation mentality is not for our future. We are all connected and what we do has an effect on humanity; all of God's creation.

Those who are bent on naming all of those have failed us and calling for a lynching are missing the opportunity to take that energy and spend it on bringing in the solution. We must take personal responsibility and become independent of needing those who prey upon the earth. Those who cannot come to peace will be dealt with by the hands of Karma and their own doing, and we should focus on repairing and bringing in a better world.

Just as a parent would not destroy their child that gets lost, then so too should we be the parent that brings in the better way that they can also choose to follow. Kindness, gentleness, respect for life, recognition of the sanctity of life is what we should be ushering into our reality. So much time has been sent on fear, hate, and control. It is time, humanity, time to let go of darkness, empower those who have failed, but are willing and embrace the love that the creator has endowed us all with, if we just stop to know it. We will not succeed if only a few stand in love, but we must come together in love and recognize that we are ready to let go of darkness.

Discernment

Discernment is a spiritual aspect of the human consciousness. It is often the difference between making wise decisions and making a miscalculated one. It is an understanding of many perspectives and understanding where components will enforce their influence. Then a choice for the sacredness of integrity and sovereignty must be expressed. Leaders must pay very close attention to their discernment development. Wise leadership is the difference between empowering development and creating a devolutionary consequence. Using discernment will either create harmony or disharmony.

Humanity is still in a lower development as a component of unison. We are yet to live in harmony with ourselves and this is a great hindrance in our presence in creation. Humanities capacity is great, but we are using a small part of that capacity as a whole. Our resources in human nature of a spiritual capacity are latent in some. Just as our schools begin educating our children on how to process information much like a computer processor, we are yet to understand the lacking of spiritual education for the human race. This spiritual development is not about a religious component, but one of character and creation. It is about a deep respect for all life and in recognizing that we are all connected. It is about living in peace with one another.

Religion

Much of our resources and efforts go into keeping a monetary system functioning, but less focus has been seriously developed to ensure the spiritual development of the human race as a whole. While world religions have sought to focus on this spiritual development, the very divide between them once again serves to separate humanity. This reason is centered in the idea of superiority and as the only way to the creator. The vast contributions that religion has given humanity then will fall short on this point. We must learn to love unconditionally.

The uses of saviors have not been reserved for those who are deserving of this title, but rather it is repeated even in our peers. There should be no savior that can keep humanity from the creator. The creator is accessible by all and from all walks of life without the necessity of allegiance to any human form. The creator is altruistic in truth and love. No human expression can rival this. No modern savior can completely carry this altruistic love without a human or other worldly agenda. This point should be remembered by every spiritual being upon this planet so that mistakes of the past will not be repeated. Hitler was given allegiance as if he was a great powerful savior by many before his true spiritual expression was realized.

We must understand that we are all connected and have a deep respect for individual expression. This is a great aspect of the human race. However, we must use discernment in how we approach our spiritual development. We should not still be dealing with issues of the carnal such as discrimination based on physical attributes, entitlement, and superiority, but should have already graduated to a place of respect and integrity. Humanity is much like a small child who has missed the bus ride to school. We must find our own way to joining the education process of humanity. This means that there must be a refocusing on discerning our efforts.

Universal truths are a shared understanding where all expressions of spirituality can share a deep respect of other expressions. Life is sacred and individual expression must be seen as sovereign. Seeking expression as long as it harms no one must be a freedom that is accepted by all. All deserve love, respect, and kindness. All of humanity should be treated as family.

Sacred Individual Expressions

The animated part of every being upon this planet is animated because of a spirit that inhabits that particular being. Each being is an expression of creation. As such, we are responsible for our expression and its interaction with others. The vast perspectives of this expression allow humanity to articulate great creativity and independence. Conformity is not the same as cooperation. Conformity is an expression of concern for what others perceive as acceptable. Learning to live in harmony does not include the stripping of individual expression, but recognizes the value of cooperation. This point must be considered sacred because without this point of discernment, history will repeat itself in harming its own kind. Functioning as one race means that humanity must recognize the value of the individual life. Without this discernment degradation will show itself.

Sacred Love of Life

Inner authority of each individual must be realized and exercised in all of our decisions. We should question all of our involvements and never seek allegiance to any other, but rather we should seek allegiance to the sacredness of acknowledging the value of each life. Deception is a daily aspect of life and discerning and navigating through this is an essential part of our spiritual growth. The lacking of its mastery is a sign of the deficient spiritual acknowledgment of life.

Those who are spiritually awakened recognize that the greater good rests on the sacredness of kindness in every interaction and in every expression of creation. They recognize that no technology, station of influence, or perceived station of power should be the determining factor of decisions. This narrow window of understanding is what separates those who are ready to lead themselves and support others in this journey of life. Exercising discernment will show a true leader from one who is pawned by outer influences.

Graduating From Fear Based Discernment

Fear is a low development expression and its influence must be outgrown in order for humanity to graduate to the next level of maturity. Decisions should not be made on fear and its presence only postures us in a weak position. It acts as an area of manipulation. Fear is a trigger where humanity can be controlled and used for other influences other than empowerment and harmony. Having concern and channeling this concern into a proactive expression is the appropriate place in discerning interaction. No matter the grave expression of a situation, we must be in a place where we do not become entangled by the power of fear. In that moment, we will become its subject, just as a pawn is predictable in a game of chess. In that moment, we are not functioning as spiritual beings, but rather as expressions of degraded emotion. This could be one of the greatest single downfalls of mankind. While fear causes submission, it also causes spiritual degradation.

Conflict

Fear has bred much conflict in humanity. Human nature has given way to fear based solutions. This has stunted the maturity of humanity. It has pitted humans against themselves. It has wasted great spiritual resources, caused spiritual degradation, and created a form of slavery within the human community. It imposes great pain upon the heart of humanity. Instead of withholding privilege by those who harm others, harm is inflicted. This is much like abusing your own child in order to get them to behave. This concept is progressive, but it is also a truth that humanity needs to come to soon or risk regret that will impact our very existence. Conflict should be handled with diplomacy and respect for those that are caught in the fold. Risking the harm of those who are innocent to enforce power as a solution only shows a great deal of disregard for discernment. Harming the innocent will only breed more conflict.

Spiritual Mastery

Intellectual intelligence is only a small part of what a leader should be. The spiritual intelligence is far more important to the existence of humanity than most have realized. The level of exposure to new challenges will commence with great consequences and those who are not prepared will be manipulated. The grief caused by this manipulation will be a great grief that could lead to the disbanding of humanity. Much like an endangered animal in the wildlife kingdom, humanity is teetering on a station in the future. The lack of this understanding is a grave weakness for humanity. Entitlement will not save humanity, but will only show others that we are in fact weak and live by our lower instincts. Then those who are entitled will then be used as pawns. They will then be in a position to take on karma of their own suppression.

Humanity must begin to recognize those who cannot reach a level of trust and empowerment away from fear in their discernment. Just because we have appointed leaders does not mean that they possess the skills and spiritual maturity to care for humanity. Our discernment must be exercised in a sacred place where we are not devotees, but rather stewards of supporting truth and individual sovereignty. We need to be selectively giving loyalty in our lives. This loyalty lies in appropriate benefits for the human race and the recognition of love for all of humanity. If we cannot be loyal to our own race, then we are still to be spiritually mature. We will be manipulated and we will regret its ending.

Wisdom Gained

Your wisdom is only as good as its application. One of the major things to be cautious of is how you can project what you want on to others. You can see things in them that may indeed be there, but they might not even realize that it is truth. This can leave you feeling as if you were taken. A deeper understanding of wisdom will dictate that wisdom is not owned, but is as universal as truth. It is the application that many of us are still seeking to apply. Wisdom exists without bias and a confused perspective. It is the responsibility of the individual to practice this wisdom even if the other person lacks its understanding.

A New Community

A new vision of one voice is moving beyond a matrix. It consists of a place of harmony and peace for humanity. It begins with thought and hope. Envision a place where energy does not harm the environment or its inhabitants. Wind, solar, and magnetic energy are readily available for everyone. Picture a place where our buildings live in conjunction with the landscape. Communities are not crowded and the clear sky is a backdrop behind the beautifully designed structures. Look closely and see a community where we care for each other and work towards a common good.

Food is grown locally and can be eaten fresh. Delicacy treats or other desirables can be obtained from other communities by trade. There are no burdening rules to pursuing one's dream and vision is shared and celebrated not controlled and taxed. Trade is also an acceptable means of commerce and it keeps all in balance. It ensures that no one become too great or that one does not participate. It relieves the stress of burdening interests.

Education is free and freely given to those who desire to evolve the spirit. Knowledge is free, open and inclusive of all past experiences. All ancient scrolls are freely read and shared. Full disclosure of truth is present to ensure the freeing of mankind. The spirit is free even as it is free today, but now the expression is even freer to express and explore. Technology is used only in harmony with nature and for the good of all. Personal responsibility is in every subject and every subject has personal responsibility as its base. Life is seen as a lifelong education filled with opportunities to learn in practical ways. Public sharing of our growth and creativity become an entertainment.

There is freedom in the days to enjoy life and spend it with the only true organization; family. Gathering of friends and community is done often and the only necessary competition is in the games and the baking of the best pastries that are at these functions. True freedom exists there in the form of health care and wellness, travel, and identity. All modalities are free to explore and illness is only an imbalance that is treated with the rebalance of natural law. Knowledge is passed down each time to each generation with great accuracy. The only limitations are the ones you might put upon yourself.

The senses are heightened with the embracing of the spirit that is living in harmony with others and nature. The human race is maturing and lessons are not based on fear and guilt, but rather on growth and lessons learned with the support of others. We evolve in spirit with our senses growing and our DNA remembering. Acknowledging that we were created with great design and that our time here is to be spent growing, learning to love, and understanding life and embracing the universe where we all live in harmony. The sanctity of life is evident and we know that what we do in this timeline to others will be reviewed from other's perspectives when we cross over. We will feel life and what we have done as if we are in their shoes. We are spiritual beings living in the flesh and everyone deserves to be respected and cherished just as our creator has done in the beautiful gifts we have been given on this planet.

Everything in nature of land, water, and tree and plant is already ours given by the creator. There is no need to pay for what is freely given to us, the creation. Therefore, time is better spent on "mindful" things of pleasure, thought, peace, and growth. Love is the ultimate goal and everyone is free to take part. Everyone has something to contribute as young and as "old". Wisdom has replaced cleverness and kindness is ordinary. We construct homes from resources that will last many generations and live in harmony with our environment. Our planet is pleased. There is no damming of water to stop the natural flow of nature, no creation of radioactive wastes, no going against nature with splitting of atoms that natural law has placed intact. There is efficiency and creations are as unusual as any imagination deems. No one is without a place and no one is without a community.

Now ask yourself what you can do to move towards this vision. How can you make it part of your reality? Think. Feel. Dare to imagine. Billions of us now have the power to create and be part of that creation. Accept empowerment from thought and explore the possibilities.

References:

Abrams, Irwin. *Nobel Lectures*, Peace 1971-1980, Editor-in-Charge Tore Frängsmyr, World Scientific Publishing Co., Singapore, 1997. Retrieved from: http://www.nobelprize.org/nobel_organizations/nobelfoundation/publications/lectures/index.html

Aitken RJ.MRC Reproductive Biology Unit, Edinburgh, UK.J Reprod Fertil 1999 Jan;115(1):1-7 Retrieved on April 5, 2009 from: http://www.ncbi.nlm.nih.gov/pubmed/10341716

Austin. Population Implosion, Graying of the Population, Population Reduction, and Negative Population Growth. Retrieved on April 5, 2009 from: http://www.population-awareness.net/older.html

Baker, B. (2008, September). HIRING HINTS. *PM Network*, *22*(9), 26-26. Retrieved April 5, 2009, from Business Source Premier database.

Coutu, D. (2009, April). Leadership Lessons from Abraham Lincoln. *Harvard Business Review*, *87*(4), 43-47. Retrieved April 4, 2009, from Business Source Premier database.

Dosa, M.D., David. (2010) Making rounds With Oscar. The Extraordinary Gift of an Ordinary Cat.

Eadie, B. 1992. Embraced by the Light. Gold Leaf Press
Eulitt, M. and Hoyer, Dr. S. 2001. Fireweaver. The Story of a Life, a Near-Death, and Beyond.Xlibris Publications.

Eveleth, D., & Pillutla, A. (2003, April). Task Demands, Task Interest, and Task Performance: Implications for Human Subjects Research and Practicing What We Preach. *Ethics & Behavior*, *13*(2), 153-172. Retrieved April 5, 2009, doi:NO_DOI

FAO, 2009. Total and agricultural population (including forestry and fisheries) Retrieved from: http://www.fao.org/docrep/014/am079m/PDF/am079m01a.pdf

Gardenswartz, L., Cherbosque, J., & Rowe, A. (2009, February). Coaching Teams: for Emotional Intelligence in Your Diverse Workplace. *T+D*, *63*(2), 44-49. Retrieved April 4, 2009, from Academic Search Premier database.

Gardner, Howard. (1983). Frames of Mind: The Theory of Multiple Intelligences. New York, Basic Books.

Georgia Guidestones. Retrieved on April 5, 2009 from: http://en.wikipedia.org/wiki/Georgia_Guidestones

Hoyer, Dr. S. 200, Vital Signs Volume XIX. Xlibris publications.

Hudley, Tom. Birth Rate In Italy Is Declining -- Changing Social Patterns Lead To Startling Demographic Shift Retrieved on April 5 2009 from: http://community.seattletimes.nwsource.com/archive/?date=19981211&slug=2788364

Kayne, R. 2011 What is String Theory? Retrieved on November 20, 2012 from: http://www.wisegeek.com/what-is-string-theory.htm

Kubler-Ross, Elisabeth On Death and Dying. New York: Macmillan, 1969.

Maslow, Abraham., THE FARTHER REACHES OF HUMAN NATURE Essays: Biology, Synergy, Creativity, Cognition, Self-Actualization, the Hierarchy of Needs, New York, New York: Penguin Books.

Moutafi, J., Furnham, A., & Crump, J. (2007, September). Is Managerial Level Related to Personality?. *British Journal of Management, 18*(3), 272-280. Retrieved April 5, 2009, doi:10.1111/j.1467-8551.2007.00511.x

Murray, Rich. DNA damage in 85% of human sperm 7.3.1 montrealgazette.com
Negative Population Growth. Frequently Asked Questions. Retrieved on April 5, 2009 from: http://www.npg.org/faq.html#anchor12Ruse

Nahavandi, A. (2006). *The art and science of leadership* (4th ed.). Upper Saddle River, NJ: Prentice-Hall.

O'Leary, B. Ph. D. (2008). The Energy Solution Revolution. Hayden, ID. Bridger House Publishers, Inc.

Personality: What Type Are You?. *RDH, 28*(5), 78-93. Retrieved April 5, 2009, from Business Source Premier database.

Population Implosion, Graying of the Population, Population Reduction, and Negative Population Growth. Retrieved on April 5, 2009 from: http://Population-awareness.net/older.html

Steensma, H. (2007, June). Why managers prefer some influence tactics to other tactics: A net utility explanation. *Journal of Occupational & Organizational Psychology, 80*(2), 355-362. Retrieved April 5, 2009, from Academic Search Premier database.

Tasler, N., & Su, L. (2009, January 19). The Emotional Ignorance Trap. *Business Week Online*, Retrieved April 4, 2009, from Academic Search Premier database.

The Great Garbage Patch. Retrieved on March 14, 2009 from: http://www.greatgarbagepatch.org/
Wall, S. (2008, May).

Williams, K. (2002) Nothing Better Than Death. Xlibris publishing.
Yeung, R. (2008, August). PERSONAL. *Accountancy, 142*(1380), 64-65. Retrieved April 5, 2009, from Business Source Premier database.

UNESCO Courier, November *1991 Retrieved from*
http://unesdoc.unesco.org/images/0009/000902/090256eo.pdf

ABOUT THE AUTHOR

Dianne Irene was born in the Northeast United States from Austro-Hungarian Empire and English heritage. Her maternal family endured parts of WWII in Europe where her grandfather Paul served as a major. Her grandparents Paul and Irene, stood in defiance of Hitler's reign and they received threats from the communists. Her grandparents, mother Csilla, and uncle Zoltan fled Austria for the United States when they were sponsored by Bert and Sally Kozma. This travesty inspired Dianne to remember the value of every human life. She now works as an advocate for human progression.

Dianne has given her time working and volunteering for various social, educational, humanitarian, and animal causes. She has worked at a private counseling facility and as a mentor at a woman's pregnancy facility, volunteered as a counselor for a battered woman's shelter, a teen prison group, for adult alcohol and drug programs, and volunteered at hospitals. She has also taught for several colleges.

She has attended seven universities or colleges which have included Kent State University, Capella University, YSU, and AIU. She has had over 15 years of experience in speaking and performing in public, on radio, and local tv. Dianne Irene has spoken for educational events, seminars, nutrition companies, and a documentary. She is a published writer and her works have appeared in newsletters, websites, and publications.

SpiritualIQ.info

Made in the USA
Charleston, SC
18 June 2015